DEBBIE BROWN'S

Cute Cakes
for Children

15 fun and colourful party cakes to make at home

This book is dedicated to my three gorgeous grandchildren, Hannah, Essie and Liam. My heart lifts every time I think of them or see them and I never thought I could love these children as much as I do. I love so many things – the sparkle in Hannah's eyes, the never-let-go hug around the neck from Essie and the cheekiest smile and best snuggles from Liam. They inspire me all the time and going back to my own childhood with them is enchanting, apart from getting stuck in playhouse doorways and sliding along floors! This book is for you, Hannah, Essie and Liam, I hope you'll look through the pages and be proud of your Nanna one day, although I doubt you could ever equal how proud I am of you. xxx

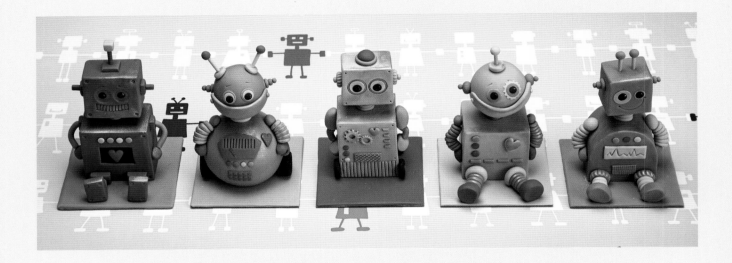

First published in October 2015 by B. Dutton Publishing Limited, The Grange, Hones Yard, Farnham, Surrey, GU9 8BB.

Copyright: Debra Brown 2015

ISBN-13: 978-1-905113-53-8

All rights reserved.

Publisher: Beverley Dutton

Group Editor: Jennifer Kelly

Art Director/Designer: Sarah Ryan

Book publishing

Copy Editor: Frankie New

Photography: Alister Thorpe

Magazine publishing

Editor: Jenny Royle

Copy Editor: Adele Duthie

Senior Graphic Designer: Zena Deakin

PR and Advertising Manager: Natalie Bull

Printed and bound in Slovenia by arrangement with Associated Agencies, Oxford

Disclaimer

The Author and Publisher have made every effort to ensure that the contents of this book, if followed carefully, will not cause harm or injury or pose any danger. Please note that some inedible items, such as lolly sticks and cake dowels, have been used in the projects in this book. All such inedible items must be removed before the cake is eaten. Similarly, any equipment and substances not approved for contact with food, such as non-toxic glue, must not come into contact with any cake or cake covering that is to be eaten. Neither the Author nor the Publisher can be held responsible for errors or omissions and cannot accept liability for injury, damage or loss to persons or property, however it may arise, as a result of acting upon guidelines and information printed in this book.

Introduction

This will be my 20th original title over a span of 25 years and I've found that what people want and expect from a cake is changing. With a plethora of information available online, people are pushing the boundaries of cake design with huge gravity-defying sculptures and, as a result, we expect to see centrepieces that are bigger and better than ever.

I bore this in mind when putting together this selection of children's birthday cakes – I know many home bakers and novice cake decorators would find it daunting to make a large sculpted centrepiece and often the cost of buying a bespoke cake can be expensive. Some cakes have been scaled up in size with the help of simple food-safe stands and supports, so the cakes look impressive but are actually straightforward to make at home. What's more, you'll only need a handful of tools so you can make a grand centrepiece that any child would love but that won't blow the budget.

The designs within this book will appeal to children of all ages; they are classic favourites across a range of popular party themes so you'll be sure to find the perfect cake to suit your celebration. I've kept some sculptures simpler than others, so busy bakers can still find the time to make an amazing centrepiece for the party table. I have also included complementary mini cakes or cupcakes with each main cake project – many of these can be scaled up to the size of the main design, giving you a broad range of designs to choose from.

As I always say, cake decorating is a wonderful creative outlet. I hope you find inspiration within these pages and that the cakes you make are enjoyed along with the special birthday celebrations, making memories that will last forever.

Debbie

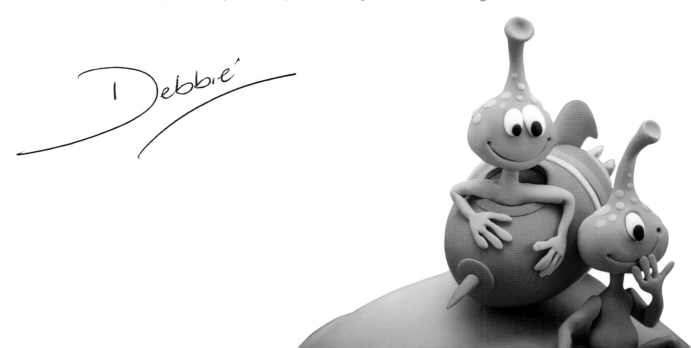

ACKNOWLEDGEMENTS

To my husband Paul, as always, for the total support and help throughout. I do appreciate you even if I don't tell you enough.

To my daughter Laura, who insisted I include more girly cakes and that they had to use pink, pink and more pink.

I always appreciate the work that goes into putting my book together, the wonderful way Alister Thorpe photographs my cakes makes them look amazing, with the help of Sarah Ryan and Frankie New. Although the camera never lies, it takes a certain skill to capture it to the best advantage. A huge thank you also to my editor, Jennifer Kelly, for looking after me and all her authors like a mother hen.

A special thank you to all my friends, fans and students around the world, I am so fortunate be able to travel to teach and see you all personally. I won't forget my friends on Facebook too, they give me a lift when I have so much work and five minutes spent connecting with them is cheering. Shenaz Lake-Thomas' and Jo Ranson's banter was very welcome just when I was struggling to find time to finish the last of the text. I feel I'm fortunate to know some very special people.

Contents

24
Stegosaurus

32
Playing Dress-Up

40
Under the Sea

50
Monster Truck

56
Puppy Love

64
Alien Encounter

72
Princess Carriage

80
Farmyard Fun

92
Friendly Robot

100
Ahoy Me Hearties!

110
Safari Friends

120
Ladybird Toadstool
House

128
Choo-Choo Train

134
Cheeky Monkeys

140
Unicorn Castle

Recipes and Baking Charts

BUTTER SPONGE CAKE

Nothing tastes quite like a butter sponge cake and it is versatile enough to complement many different flavours and fillings. This recipe has a little extra flour to make it slightly firmer for sculpting and the addition of buttermilk makes the sponge moist with a rich and smooth taste. You can also moisten the cake further by brushing the layers with sugar syrup (see page 10).

1 Preheat the oven to 150°C/300°F/gas mark 2, then grease and line the bakeware.

2 Sift the self-raising flour into a bowl.

3 Soften the butter and place it in a food mixer or large mixing bowl with the caster/superfine sugar. Beat until the mixture is pale and fluffy.

4 Add the eggs to the mixture one at a time with a spoonful of the flour, beating well after each addition.

5 Using a spatula or large spoon, fold the remaining flour into the mixture.

6 Gently stir in the vanilla extract and buttermilk.

7 Spoon the mixture into the bakeware then make a dip in the top of the mixture using the back of a spoon. If you are using more than one tin, make sure each one is evenly filled; if you are making cupcakes, ½- to ¾-fill each cupcake case.

8 Bake in the centre of the oven for the recommended time or until a skewer inserted in the centre comes out clean.

9 Leave to cool in the bakeware for five minutes, then turn out onto a wire rack and leave to cool completely. When cold, store in an airtight container or double wrap in cling film (plastic wrap) for at least eight hours, allowing the texture to settle before use.

Basic variations for butter sponge cake

Chocolate marble cake
Before spooning the cake mixture into the bakeware, fold in 200g (7oz) of melted chocolate until marbled. For a light chocolate cake, fold in the chocolate completely.

Chocolate orange marble cake
Make as per the chocolate marble cake and add the grated rind and juice of one organic orange.

Lemon cake
Add the grated rind and juice of one organic lemon to the cake mixture.

Orange and lemon cake
Add the grated rind of an organic orange and lemon to the cake mixture and a squeeze of orange juice.

Coffee cake
Add 2 tablespoons of coffee essence to the cake mixture.

Almond cake
Add 1 teaspoon of almond essence and 2–3 tablespoons of ground almonds to the cake mixture.

Cake project	Bakeware	Unsalted butter, softened	Caster (superfine) sugar, sifted	Large eggs	Self-raising flour, sifted	Vanilla extract	Buttermilk	Baking time
20 cupcakes	Cupcake cases	225g (8oz)	225g (8oz)	4	225g (8oz)	1tsp	15ml (1tbsp)	20 minutes
6 spherical mini cakes	12 x 7cm (3") half-sphere tins/moulds/ovenproof bowls	170g (5¾oz)	170g (5¾oz)	3	215g (7¾oz)	1tsp	15ml (1tbsp)	30 minutes
Stegosaurus	1 x 20cm (8") half-sphere tin/ovenproof bowl and 1 x 20cm (8") round tin	340g (12oz)	340g (12oz)	6	430g (15oz)	1tsp	55ml (3tbsp)	1–1¼ hours
Playing Dress-Up	2 x 15cm (6") and 2 x 10cm (4") round tins, 1 x mini loaf tin	340g (12oz)	340g (12oz)	6	430g (15oz)	1tsp	55ml (3tbsp)	1–1¼ hours for 15cm (6") and 10cm (4") and 20 minutes for mini loaf tin
Under the Sea	2 x 15cm (6"), 2 x 10cm (4") and 2 x 7cm (3") half-sphere tins/moulds/ovenproof bowls	455g (1lb)	455g (1lb)	8	565g (1lb 4oz)	1tsp	75ml (4tbsp)	1–1¼ hours for 15cm (6"), 50 minutes–1 hour for 10cm (4") and 30 minutes for 7cm (3")
Monster Truck	1 x 15cm (6") and 2 x 7cm (3") half-sphere tins/moulds/ovenproof bowls, 1 x 20cm (8") square tin	340g (12oz)	340g (12oz)	6	430g (15oz)	1tsp	55ml (3tbsp)	1–1¼ hours for 15cm (6"), 30 minutes for 7cm (3") and 50 minutes–1 hour for 20cm (8") square
Puppy Love	2 x 15cm (6") and 4 x 7cm (3") half-sphere tins/moulds/ovenproof bowls	455g (1lb)	455g (1lb)	8	565g (1lb 4oz)	1tsp	75ml (4tbsp)	1–1¼ hours for 15cm (6") and 30 minutes for 7cm (3")
Alien Encounter	1 x 20cm (8") half-sphere tin/ovenproof bowl and 1 x 20cm (8") round tin	340g (12oz)	340g (12oz)	6	430g (15oz)	1tsp	55ml (3tbsp)	1–1¼ hours
Princess Carriage	1 x 20cm (8") half-sphere tin/ovenproof bowl and 1 x 20cm (8") round tin	340g (12oz)	340g (12oz)	6	430g (15oz)	1tsp	55ml (3tbsp)	1–1¼ hours
Farmyard Fun	1 x 30cm (12") square tin	520g (1lb 2oz)	520g (1lb 2oz)	9	565g (1lb 4oz)	2tsp	90ml (5tbsp)	1–1¼ hours
Friendly Robot	3 x 15cm (6") square tins	455g (1lb)	455g (1lb)	8	565g (1lb 4oz)	1tsp	75ml (4tbsp)	1–1¼ hours
Ahoy Me Hearties!	1 x 20cm (8") half-sphere tin/ovenproof bowl and 2 x 20cm (8") round tins	455g (1lb)	455g (1lb)	8	565g (1lb 4oz)	1tsp	75ml (4tbsp)	1–1¼ hours
Safari Friends	2 x 15cm (6") and 2 x 7cm (3") half-sphere tins/moulds/ovenproof bowls	455g (1lb)	455g (1lb)	8	565g (1lb 4oz)	1tsp	75ml (4tbsp)	1–1¼ hours for 15cm (6") and 30 minutes for 7cm (3")
Ladybird Toadstool House	1 x 20cm (8"), 1 x 15cm (6") and 1 x 10cm (4") round tins	520g (1lb 2oz)	520g (1lb 2oz)	9	565g (1lb 4oz)	2tsp	90ml (5tbsp)	1–1¼ hours
Choo-Choo Train	2 x 20cm (8") square tins	455g (1lb)	455g (1lb)	8	565g (1lb 4oz)	1tsp	75ml (4tbsp)	1–1¼ hours
Cheeky Monkeys	2 x 20cm (8") round tins	340g (12oz)	340g (12oz)	6	430g (15oz)	1tsp	55ml (3tbsp)	1–1¼ hours
Unicorn Castle	2 x 15cm (6") and 2 x 10cm (4") round tins	455g (1lb)	455g (1lb)	8	565g (1lb 4oz)	1tsp	75ml (4tbsp)	1–1¼ hours

DEVIL'S CHOCOLATE CAKE

This recipe won't disappoint as it bakes well with an even and easy-to-sculpt texture that keeps exceptionally rich and moist.

1 Preheat the oven to 160°C/325°F/gas mark 3.

2 Make the coffee in a heat-resistant bowl. Break the dark chocolate into small pieces, add to the coffee and stir until melted. Leave to cool.

3 Beat the softened butter and dark brown sugar together until light and fluffy. Gradually add the eggs one at a time, then stir in the vanilla extract and the cooled chocolate/coffee mixture.

4 Sift the plain flour and bicarbonate of soda together and gradually fold into the mixture a little at a time until well blended and the mixture is smooth. Stir in the soured cream.

5 Spoon the mixture into the bakeware then make a dip in the top of the mixture using the back of a spoon. If you are using more than one tin, make sure each one is evenly filled; if you are making cupcakes, ½- to ¾-fill each cupcake case.

6 Bake in the centre of the oven for the recommended time or until a skewer inserted in the centre comes out clean.

7 Leave to cool in the bakeware for five minutes, then turn out onto a wire rack and leave to cool completely. When cold, store in an airtight container or double wrap in cling film (plastic wrap) for at least eight hours, allowing the texture to settle before use.

Cake project	Bakeware	Hot, strong black coffee	Dark couverture chocolate	Unsalted butter, softened	Soft, dark brown sugar	Large eggs	Vanilla extract	Plain flour (sifted)	Bicarbonate of soda	Soured cream	Baking time
30 cupcakes	Cupcake cases	175ml (6fl oz)	75g (2½oz)	175g (6oz)	280g (9¾oz)	3	1tsp	280g (9¾oz)	1½tsp	175ml (6fl oz)	20 minutes
6 spherical mini cakes	12 x 7cm (3") half-sphere tins/moulds/ovenproof bowls	120ml (4¼fl oz)	75g (2½oz)	120g (4¼oz)	185g (6½oz)	2	1tsp	185g (6½oz)	1tsp	120ml (4¼fl oz)	30 minutes
Stegosaurus	1 x 20cm (8") half-sphere tin/ovenproof bowl and 1 x 20cm (8") round tin	235ml (8¼fl oz)	175g (6oz)	235g (8¼oz)	375g (13¼oz)	4	2tsp	375g (13¼oz)	2tsp	235ml (8¼fl oz)	1–1¼ hours
Playing Dress-Up	2 x 15cm (6") and 2 x 10cm (4") round tins, 1 x mini loaf tin	235ml (8¼fl oz)	175g (6oz)	235g (8¼oz)	375g (13¼oz)	4	2tsp	375g (13¼oz)	2tsp	235ml (8¼fl oz)	1–1¼ hours for 15cm (6") and 10cm (4"), 20 minutes for mini loaf tin
Under the Sea	2 x 15cm (6"), 2 x 10cm (4") and 2 x 7cm (3") half-sphere tins/moulds/ovenproof bowls	350ml (12¼fl oz)	225g (8oz)	350g (12¼oz)	550g (1lb 3½oz)	6	2tsp	550g (1lb 3½oz)	3tsp	350ml (12¼fl oz)	1–1¼ hours for 15cm (6"), 50 minutes–1 hour for 10cm (4") and 30 minutes for 7cm (3")
Monster Truck	1 x 15cm (6") and 2 x 7cm (3") half-sphere tins/moulds/ovenproof bowls, 1 x 20cm (8") square tin	235ml (8¼fl oz)	175g (6oz)	235g (8¼oz)	375g (13¼oz)	4	2tsp	375g (13¼oz)	2tsp	235ml (8¼fl oz)	1–1¼ hours for 15cm (6"), 30 minutes for 7cm (3") and 50 minutes–1 hour for 20cm (8") square
Puppy Love	2 x 15cm (6") and 4 x 7cm (3") half-sphere tins/moulds/ovenproof bowls	350ml (12¼fl oz)	225g (8oz)	350g (12¼oz)	550g (1lb 3½oz)	6	2tsp	550g (1lb 3½oz)	3tsp	350ml (12¼fl oz)	1–1¼ hours for 15cm (6") and 30 minutes for 7cm (3")
Alien Encounter	1 x 20cm (8") half-sphere tin/ovenproof bowl and 1 x 20cm (8") round tin	235ml (8¼fl oz)	175g (6oz)	235g (8¼oz)	375g (13¼oz)	4	2tsp	375g (13¼oz)	2tsp	235ml (8¼fl oz)	1–1¼ hours
Princess Carriage	1 x 20cm (8") half-sphere tin/ovenproof bowl and 1 x 20cm (8") round tin	235ml (8¼fl oz)	175g (6oz)	235g (8¼oz)	375g (13¼oz)	4	2tsp	375g (13¼oz)	2tsp	235ml (8¼fl oz)	1–1¼ hours
Farmyard Fun	1 x 30cm (12") square tin	350ml (12¼fl oz)	225g (8oz)	350g (12¼oz)	550g (1lb 3½oz)	6	2tsp	550g (1lb 3½oz)	3tsp	350ml (12¼fl oz)	1–1¼ hours
Friendly Robot	3 x 15cm (6") square tins	350ml (12¼fl oz)	225g (8oz)	350g (12¼oz)	550g (1lb 3½oz)	6	2tsp	550g (1lb 3½oz)	3tsp	350ml (12¼fl oz)	1–1¼ hours
Ahoy Me Hearties!	1 x 20cm (8") half-sphere tin/ovenproof bowl and 2 x 20cm (8") round tins	350ml (12¼fl oz)	225g (8oz)	350g (12¼oz)	550g (1lb 3½oz)	6	2tsp	550g (1lb 3½oz)	3tsp	350ml (12¼fl oz)	1–1¼ hours
Safari Friends	2 x 15cm (6") and 2 x 7cm (3") half-sphere tins/moulds/ovenproof bowls	350ml (12¼fl oz)	225g (8oz)	350g (12¼oz)	550g (1lb 3½oz)	6	2tsp	550g (1lb 3½oz)	3tsp	350ml (12¼fl oz)	1–1¼ hours for 15cm (6") and 30 minutes for 7cm (3")
Ladybird Toadstool House	1 x 20cm (8"), 1 x 15cm (6") and 1 x 10cm (4") round tins	350ml (12¼fl oz)	225g (8oz)	350g (12¼oz)	550g (1lb 3½oz)	6	2tsp	550g (1lb 3½oz)	3tsp	350ml (12¼fl oz)	1–1¼ hours
Choo-Choo Train	2 x 20cm (8") square tins	350ml (12¼fl oz)	225g (8oz)	350g (12¼oz)	550g (1lb 3½oz)	6	2tsp	550g (1lb 3½oz)	3tsp	350ml (12¼fl oz)	1–1¼ hours
Cheeky Monkeys	2 x 20cm (8") round tins	235ml (8¼fl oz)	175g (6oz)	235g (8¼oz)	375g (13¼oz)	4	2tsp	375g (13¼oz)	2tsp	235ml (8¼fl oz)	1–1¼ hours
Unicorn Castle	2 x 15cm (6") and 2 x 10cm (4") round tins	350ml (12¼fl oz)	225g (8oz)	350g (12¼oz)	550g (1lb 3½oz)	6	2tsp	550g (1lb 3½oz)	3tsp	350ml (12¼fl oz)	1–1¼ hours

SUGAR SYRUP (MOISTENING SYRUP)

For butter sponge cake and variations

Sugar syrup is an easy way to ensure your cake remains moist during the preparation process and, of course, the serving. When preparing your cake for decorating, brush or dab sugar syrup carefully over each sponge cake layer, preferably with a silicone pastry brush before the cake filling is added. The syrup slowly soaks into the sponge until it is distributed evenly throughout the cake. I also brush syrup over the top and sides of the sponge cake just before the crumb-coat is spread over the surface as I find it spreads a little easier.

Some cake decorators prefer to be generous when brushing on the syrup whilst others are more conservative – it purely depends on personal choice. I find excessive sugar syrup can cause the sponge to become very sweet, so I recommend the following quantity for a 25cm (10") cake. You can, of course, add more; in fact, many cake decorators use double this quantity.

Ingredients

115g (4oz) caster (superfine) sugar

125ml (4½fl oz) water

5ml (1tsp) flavouring (optional)

Makes 240ml (8½fl oz)

1 Pour the measured sugar into a saucepan along with the water. Heat gently and bring to the boil, stirring carefully. Do not leave unattended as sugar can burn easily. Simmer for one minute to ensure all the sugar granules have dissolved completely. Remove from the heat and set aside to cool.

2 Store in an airtight container and refrigerate. Use within one month.

3 Flavouring sugar syrup is not absolutely necessary but if you've baked a flavoured sponge cake then flavouring the sugar syrup to complement it can really enhance the taste. Although the most popular flavouring is vanilla, different seedless fruit jams also work very well.

BUTTERCREAM

A great versatile filling and the first choice for many, buttercream made with real unsalted butter is delicious as I find the flavour much creamier than when using salted butter. I add milk as this makes the buttercream paler in colour and much lighter in texture, but if you prefer a firmer, yellow buttercream you can omit the milk and add a little less icing sugar. The basic recipe can be flavoured if required to suit your preference.

Ingredients

175g (6oz) unsalted butter, softened

30–45ml (2–3tbsp) milk

1tsp flavouring (optional)

450g (1lb) icing sugar, sifted

Makes approximately 625g (1lb 6oz)

1 Place the softened butter, milk and flavouring into a mixer. Mix on medium speed and add the icing sugar a little at a time. Mix until light, fluffy and pale in colour.

2 Store in an airtight container and use within 10 days. Bring to room temperature and beat again before use.

Basic variations for buttercream

Chocolate

Fold in 145–200g (5–7oz) of melted and cooled dark, milk or white chocolate.

Orange or lemon

Add 30–45ml (2–3 level tbsp) of orange or lemon curd.

Coffee

Add 30–45ml (2–3tbsp) of coffee essence.

Raspberry

Add 30–45ml (2–3 level tbsp) of seedless raspberry jam.

Almond

Add 1tsp of almond essence.

SWISS MERINGUE BUTTERCREAM

Swiss meringue takes a little more time and patience to make but its stability and wonderful creamy taste makes it worth it. Make sure all ingredients are weighed carefully and are at room temperature before you begin.

Ingredients

90g (3oz) egg whites (around 2–3 egg whites)

170g (5¾oz) caster (superfine) sugar

230g (8¼oz) unsalted butter, cubed and softened

1tsp vanilla extract

Makes approximately 400–420g (14–14¾oz)

1 Place the egg whites into the bowl of a stand mixer fitted with a whisk attachment and whisk in the sugar.

2 Place the bowl over a pan of shallow, hot (but not boiling) water and allow the water to simmer. Whisk the mixture slowly until it reaches 66°C (150°F), using a sugar thermometer to measure the temperature. Ensure the sugar has completely dissolved.

3 Put the bowl back on the stand mixer and whisk the mixture on medium speed for two minutes, then whisk on a high speed for seven to eight minutes to make a meringue. Turn off the mixer and leave until the outside of the bowl is cool but not cold to the touch, whisking occasionally.

TIP

Don't be tempted to add the butter until the meringue mixture has cooled down otherwise it will curdle.

4 Fit the mixer with a paddle attachment and beat the mixture on a medium speed. Add the cubes of butter one at a time until it is all incorporated. Turn the mixer up to a high speed and mix for five minutes until the mixture has a silky-smooth texture. Add the vanilla extract and mix well.

5 Store in an airtight container in the refrigerator for up to two weeks.

MARSHMALLOW RICE CEREAL

This is not only a quick and easy, bake-free recipe that makes delicious treats, but it is also used by cake decorators as a substitute for cake in small areas of a particular design that need to be lightweight but still strong. Cake with filling can be heavy and may cause pressure and possible damage to the cake below it.

This recipe can also be used for some of the mini projects throughout the book, especially the ball-shaped designs, as it's easy to roll and when left to set is a sturdy but tasty treat that is easy to decorate.

Ingredients

50g (1¾oz) unsalted butter

200g (7oz) white marshmallows

160g (5½oz) crisped rice cereal

Makes approximately 350–380g (12¼–13½oz)

1 Melt the butter in large saucepan over a low heat. Add the marshmallows and stir constantly until melted. Stir for a further minute. Remove from the heat, add the cereal and stir until well coated.

2 Allow to cool slightly and then mould into the required shape, compacting it by pressing firmly to create a smooth surface. You will need to work quickly before it sets hard.

CHOCOLATE GANACHE

I love chocolate ganache as a filling, but it's also invaluable for crumb-coating a cake as it sets much firmer than other cake fillings. This means there is less risk of encountering problems such as bulging layers or leaning cakes. I try to keep softer fillings, such as buttercream, for the simpler designs and use ganache for larger or more complex cake sculptures.

The basic ingredients of chocolate ganache are chocolate (either dark, milk or white) and cream (either whipping or double). Always use couverture chocolate for best results, as this will melt easily unlike some of the lower-quality brands that contain less cocoa butter. The ratios of chocolate to cream differ depending on the type of chocolate you are using – dark chocolate has the highest cocoa solids content so you will need more cream. Depending on the climate and how firm you need the crumb-coat to set, I recommend a ratio of 1:1, 2:1 or 3:1 dark chocolate to cream. For cake sculptures I usually use a ratio of 2:1, but if it's a warm day or I'm making an extra-tall cake then I would probably use a ratio of 3:1 dark chocolate to cream.

I recommend a ratio of 3:1 for milk chocolate ganache and 4:1 for white chocolate ganache. Both milk and white chocolate ganache can be temperamental as the temperature has to be just right to combine the chocolate and cream together successfully. If the cream or chocolate is too hot, then the mixture can separate and have an oily, curdled texture. If this happens, just allow the ganache to cool further then keep whisking. If the mixture still doesn't combine properly try adding a few drops of warm milk and repeat, whisking gently until the mixture is smooth.

A simple alternative to making up a small amount of ganache is to use white chocolate melted to a spreadable consistency. As white chocolate ganache can be temperamental, I always recommend using melted white couverture chocolate as a crumb-coat instead. It melts beautifully and the white chocolate is paler than dark or milk, so won't show through the sugarpaste covering.

Recipe

1 Melt the chocolate in a bowl over a pan of hot water (or a bain-marie) to 40°C (105°F).

2 Pour the cream into a saucepan and bring to a simmer for two to three minutes. Allow the cream to cool slightly for approximately five minutes then whisk the cream into the melted chocolate until well combined. The mixture should be thick and glossy.

3 Allow the ganache to cool completely then transfer into an airtight container and refrigerate. Use within one month.

TIP

If you make ganache in advance and re-melt it, be careful not to heat it too much otherwise it can separate and become oily. Dark chocolate is easier to work with but milk and white need extra care, so warm these at 10-second intervals in a microwave and stir each time to ensure the mixture doesn't separate.

Approx. amount of ganache	Dark chocolate ganache		Milk chocolate ganache		White chocolate ganache	
	Dark chocolate	Double/ whipping cream	Milk chocolate	Double/ whipping cream	White chocolate	Double/ whipping cream
200g (7oz)	170g (5¾oz)	85ml (2¾fl oz)	180g (6¼oz)	60ml (2fl oz)	190g (6¾oz)	50ml (1¾fl oz)
250g (8¾oz)	190g (6¾oz)	95ml (3¼fl oz)	210g (7½oz)	70ml (2½fl oz)	240g (8½oz)	60ml (2fl oz)
350g (12¼oz)	280g (9¾oz)	140ml (5fl oz)	300g (10½oz)	100ml (3½fl oz)	320g (11¼oz)	80ml (2½fl oz)
400g (14oz)	300g (10½oz)	150ml (5¼fl oz)	360g (12½oz)	120ml (4¼fl oz)	380g (13½oz)	95ml (3¼fl oz)
550g (1lb 3½oz)	400g (14oz)	200ml (7fl oz)	465g (1lb ¼oz)	155ml (5½fl oz)	480g (1lb 1oz)	120ml (4¼fl oz)
600g (1lb 5¼oz)	450g (1lb)	225ml (8fl oz)	500g (1lb 1¾oz)	165ml (5¾fl oz)	540g (1lb 3oz)	135ml (4¾fl oz)
Ratio of chocolate to cream	2:1		3:1		4:1	

SUGARPASTE (ROLLED FONDANT)

Sugarpaste (also known as rolled fondant) is readily available throughout the UK in supermarkets and cake decorating outlets. Each brand has a slightly different texture, taste and working quality, so try different brands to find which suits you best. If you prefer to make your own, I would recommend the recipe below.

Ingredients

1 egg white made up from dried egg albumen

30ml (2tbsp) liquid glucose

625g (1lb 6oz) icing (confectioners') sugar

A little white vegetable fat (shortening), if required

A pinch of CMC powder*

Makes 625g (1lb 6oz)

*NOTE: CMC is an abbreviation of Carboxy Methyl Cellulose, an edible thickener widely used in the food industry. The CMC you use must be food grade. Brand names include Squires Kitchen CMC, Debbie Brown's Magic Powder (CMC), Tylose, Tylopur, Tylo and Sugarcel. Alternatively, you can use Squires Kitchen Gum Tragacanth, which is a natural product.

1 Put the egg white and liquid glucose into a bowl, using a warm spoon for the liquid glucose.

2 Sift the icing sugar into the bowl, adding a little at a time and stirring until the mixture thickens.

3 Turn the mixture out onto a work surface dusted liberally with icing sugar and knead the paste until soft, smooth and pliable. If the paste is slightly dry and cracked, fold in a little white vegetable fat and knead again. If the paste is very soft and sticky, add a little more icing sugar. Add a pinch of CMC to strengthen the paste.

4 Transfer the paste immediately into a food-grade polythene bag and store in an airtight container. Keep the paste cool, either at room temperature, or in the refrigerator if the atmosphere is warm. Bring back to room temperature and knead thoroughly before use.

TIP

To save time when decorating a cake, homemade sugarpaste can be frozen for up to three months. Allow to defrost thoroughly at room temperature before use.

ROYAL ICING

Royal icing is used to pipe fine details and to stick sugar pieces together: when dry it will hold items firmly in place. Ready-made royal icing can be obtained from supermarkets or in powder form (follow the instructions on the packet). If you prefer to make your own, you can follow this recipe.

Ingredients

1 level tsp egg albumen

15ml (3tsp) cooled, boiled water

65–70g (2¼oz) icing (confectioners') sugar

Makes 75g (2½oz)

1 Put the egg albumen into a bowl. Add the water and stir until dissolved.

2 Beat in the icing sugar a little at a time until the icing is firm, glossy and forms peaks if a spoon is pulled out.

3 To stop the icing forming a crust, place a damp cloth over the top of the bowl until you are ready to use it or transfer to an airtight container and refrigerate.

MODELLING PASTE

This quick and easy recipe makes a high-quality modelling paste. If you are short of time or prefer to use a ready-made paste, SK Fairtrade Sugar Modelling Paste is ready-to-use and gives good results.

Ingredients

450g (1lb) sugarpaste
1 level tsp CMC powder

Makes 450g (1lb)

Knead the CMC into the sugarpaste. The sugarpaste will start to thicken as soon as the CMC is incorporated so can be used immediately. The paste will continue to thicken gradually over a period of 24 hours. The amount of CMC can be varied depending on usage and on the room temperature and humidity, so adjust accordingly to achieve the required consistency. Store in an airtight container.

EDIBLE GLUE

This recipe makes a strong sugar glue which works extremely well. Alternatively, ready-made sugar glue can be purchased from specialist cake decorating outlets.

Ingredients

¼tsp CMC powder
30ml (2tbsp) boiled water, cooled until warm

Makes 30ml (2tbsp)

1 Mix the CMC powder with the warm water and leave to stand until the powder has fully dissolved. The glue should be smooth and have a soft dropping consistency. If the glue thickens after a few days, add a few more drops of pre-boiled water.

2 Store in an airtight container in the refrigerator and use within one week.

3 To use, brush a thin coat over the surface of the item you wish to glue, leave for a few moments to become tacky, then press the item in place.

PASTILLAGE SUGAR STICKS

These are cut or rolled lengths of pastillage, a fast-drying paste that keeps its shape and dries extremely hard. Sugar sticks are used as edible supports, mainly to help hold modelled heads in place. If you are short of time, you can use strands of dried, raw spaghetti for smaller pieces or paper lolly sticks where more support is required. Whichever option you choose, remember to remove the supports before the figures are eaten.

Ingredients

1 level tsp royal icing, made to stiff-peak consistency
¼tsp CMC
Icing sugar in sugar shaker

Makes approximately 10–20 sugar sticks

1 Mix the CMC into the royal icing until the mixture thickens and forms a paste. If the paste is slightly wet, knead in a little icing sugar until the paste is soft and pliable.

2 Either roll out the paste and cut into different-sized strips of various lengths using a plain-bladed knife, or roll individual sausages of paste to the sizes required. Leave to dry, preferably overnight on a sheet of food-grade foam sponge. When completely dry, store in an airtight container.

TIP

These can be used instead of paper lolly sticks wherever they are listed in the book. Do bear in mind, however, that the lolly sticks are slightly stronger so will support more weight and, unlike sugar, they do not absorb moisture when working in humidity.

Basic Equipment

There is a wide variety of equipment available to help you achieve brilliant results with your cake designs. If you already have sugarcraft tools or you have a good local supplier, please feel free to make the most of the items you have. I am well-known for not using much equipment, and I always bear in mind that there may be readers from other countries who may not have the choice that we have here in the UK. I usually only use what is absolutely necessary and specialist equipment that I would highly recommend – items that I use over and over again which are favourites in my small workbox.

Each project gives a list of what you will require to decorate the cake, but the items here will give you the basics to get started. A list of recommended suppliers is given on page 152.

BAKING

1 Cake leveller

2 Cupcake cases

3 Heatproof glass bowls

4 Round and square cake tins

5 Round mini cake pans

6 Mini loaf tins

7 Silicone half-sphere moulds

8 Silicone pastry brush

9 Spherical cake tin

10 Stainless steel bowls

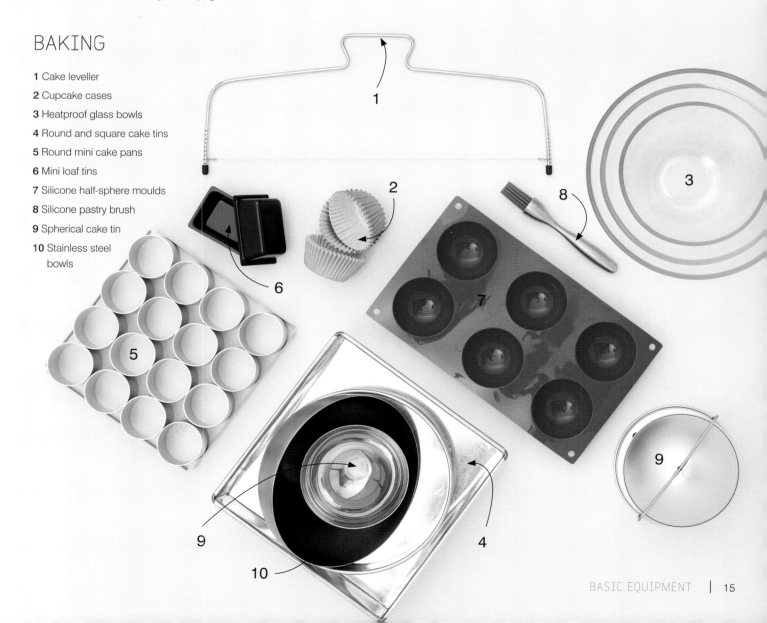

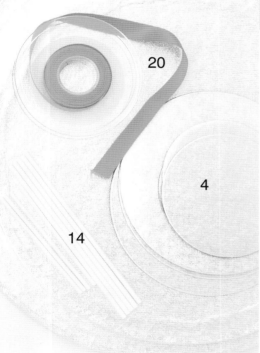

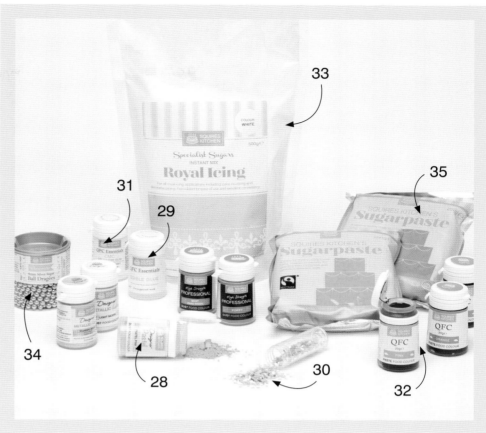

CAKE DECORATING EQUIPMENT AND EDIBLES

1 Ball tool

2 Bone tool

3 CelStick: medium

4 Cake cards

5 Cake drums (boards)

6 Cake smoothers

7 Cocktail sticks

8 Dresden tool

9 Fine scissors

10 Icing (confectioners') sugar in a
sugar shaker

11 Non-stick board

12 Paintbrushes: nos. 2, 3, 4, 6 and 10

13 Palette knives: straight and cranked

14 Paper lolly sticks

15 Paper piping bags

16 Piping nozzles

17 Plain-bladed sharp knife

18 Plastic or wooden cake dowels

19 Rolling pins: large and small

20 Ribbon

21 Ruler

22 Serrated carving knife

23 Set of round cutters, up to 10cm (4")
diameter

24 Side scraper

25 Small square, round, star and heart cutters

26 Texture mat

27 Turntable

28 Dust (powder) food colours

29 Edible glue

30 Edible sparkles or glitter

31 CMC (cellulose gum)

32 Paste food colours

33 Royal icing mix

34 Silver dragées

35 Sugarpaste

CAKE SUPPORTS

You can make amazing cake sculptures without any internal supports but some more adventurous designs benefit from their use. For instance, a seated robot design would make a great centrepiece but a standing robot would be even more impressive (see page 92). Most of the cakes in this book have been carefully designed so that they only use minimal internal supports. However, I wanted to introduce you to the different support systems available so you can be confident at making your own gravity-defying cakes at home.

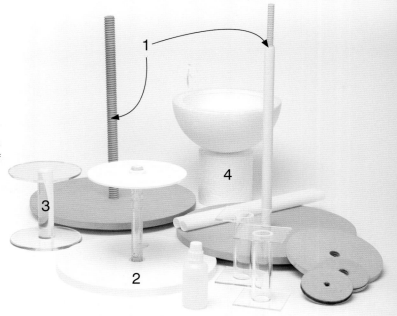

1 Threaded pole stand

This is a basic internal support with a single threaded dowel secured into a threaded hole in the centre of a double-thickness base. I like to use a threaded dowel as this means you don't have to use screws to secure the dowel in place: it simply twists into the threaded hole and is held securely by the thick base. I have used this type of support in the Ladybird Toadstool House on page 120, where the cake is sitting on an MDF support board that has been threaded in position on the dowel.

Bespoke stands are available to order from specialist companies, such as Fabricaking It. No part of the MDF stand should come into contact with the cake so it needs to be covered with a food-safe covering, such as cake board foil paper. To cover the central dowel, I recommend placing a hollow, food-safe plastic dowel over it; the ones pictured here are from Wilton.

2 Internal support kits

There are several companies which produce food-safe cake support kits, such as CakeFrame, that have multiple components so you can build your own internal structure. Whatever your design, you can use these kits to add support virtually anywhere you need it but it is still important to make sure the cake is evenly balanced. These can be expensive but are a good investment if you make cakes regularly as they can be washed and re-used many times.

3 Acrylic cake separators

Cake separators are most commonly used in traditional tiered cakes, but they are also ideal for supporting certain gravity-defying cake designs. I have used acrylic separators when a cake design needs height and has decoration underneath which disguises the supports, such as the Friendly Robot cake (see page 92).

Although the acrylic is actually washable and food-safe, the glue used to assemble the separators is not, so they shouldn't come into contact with any part of the cake which is going to be eaten. You can either purchase standard sizes online or order bespoke, either way the cost

isn't too high. If you prefer, you can purchase the tops and bases pre-cut from acrylic sheets and the hollow tubes in different thicknesses then assemble them yourself with specialist glue for plastics. I have used acrylic that is approximately 3mm (1/8") thick for both the sheets and tubes.

4 Polystyrene cake dummies

Cake dummies make great internal supports as they are lightweight and available in many different shapes and sizes. They can be sculpted to shape using a sharp knife if required and can be used as an integral part of the actual cake sculpture, as seen in the Stegosaurus cake (see page 24). To protect the cake from the chemicals within the polystyrene, make sure to place a cake card between the cake and the dummy, sticking the cake card in place with royal icing.

Important note: Be careful when sourcing your products for cake decoration: all must be food-safe and purchased from reputable companies. Please don't be tempted to pop along to your local builders' merchant and purchase a length of dowelling to use in a cake. Products purchased from DIY stores, for example, would most probably have been treated with chemicals and are not safe for direct contact with food. If you only need a simple cake dowel for support, there are many cake decoration companies that sell food-safe plastic and wooden dowels; if you do not have a supplier nearby these are easily obtainable online.

The same goes for homemade cake stands. If you decide to make your own cake stand, each surface must be made food-safe with the use of cake board paper (food-safe foil paper), or protected by a cake card. If you decide to use cake board paper, I recommend sticking it in place with royal icing so you don't need to use glue.

Basic Techniques

All of the projects in this book require the cake to be layered, filled and crumb-coated with your chosen filling (see pages 10 to 12). Following these basic instructions will give you a level surface on which to work, allowing you to achieve the best possible results when the cake is decorated. I have also given guidelines for a few other basic cake decorating techniques to help you achieve great results.

PREPARING A SPONGE CAKE

1 Trim the crust from the cake and level the top with a serrated knife or cake leveller. Cut two to four layers in the cake (a quick and easy way is to use a cake leveller, which can also be used to cut as many layers as you wish extremely easily) and brush each layer with sugar syrup to keep it moist (see page 10). Sandwich the layers together with cake filling, up to 5mm (just under ¼") deep.

2 Brush more sugar syrup over the surface of the cake before applying the crumb-coat.

3 Using a large palette knife, spread an even layer of cake filling over the surface of the cake. Spread evenly to fill any gaps and create a smooth surface. If crumbs start to appear, add a little more filling and skim over the top surface.

4 Leave the cake to firm or refrigerate until you are ready to cover it with sugarpaste (see page 20). Prior to covering, rework the crumb-coat with the palette knife to make it soft enough for the sugarpaste to stick, or brush a little sugar syrup over the surface.

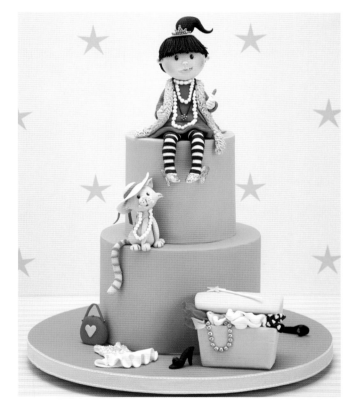

COVERING A CAKE WITH SUGARPASTE

All-in-one method (suitable for most cakes):

1 Knead the required amount of sugarpaste on a non-stick board dusted with icing sugar. Keep rotating the paste to create an even shape and ensure that it doesn't stick to the board. Do not turn the paste over as the icing sugar underneath may mark the surface.

2 Use a large rolling pin to roughly measure the cake covering area (i.e. across the top and down the sides) and roll out the paste to the required size with a thickness of around 3mm (1/8").

3 Lightly sprinkle the top of the sugarpaste with icing sugar to prevent sticking. To lift the paste, gently place the rolling pin in the centre and lightly fold the paste back over the rolling pin. This will prevent the paste from stretching and tearing. Lift carefully and position over the cake.

4 Smooth the covering down and around the cake with the palm of your hand, pressing gently around the sides to remove any air bubbles.

5 When you have smoothed over the top and sides of the cake, trim away the excess paste from around the base of the cake using a plain-bladed knife. Rub the surface gently with a cake smoother to remove any imperfections and achieve a smooth surface. After smoothing the sides, you may need to trim around the base once again to create a neat edge.

6 If you need to work on the sugarpaste while it is still soft, do this straight away. Otherwise, leave the sugarpaste for several hours as this will give you a firm surface on which to work.

TIP

As soon as you take sugarpaste out of its airtight packaging it will start to dry, so always knead it thoroughly then roll out or shape it as quickly as possible. Re-seal any trimmings in a food-grade polythene bag and keep any spare paste wrapped tightly and stored in an airtight container.

Top and sides separately (suitable for cakes where sharp edges are required):

1 Roll out the sugarpaste as described in step 1 of the all-in-one method. This time, instead of rolling out the sugarpaste big enough to cover the whole cake, roll out a piece only the size of the area you wish to cover. Cut a neat shape, using a template if necessary or measuring carefully with a ruler.

2 Using a palette knife, carefully lift the paste to avoid tearing or distorting the shape and apply to the cake. Trim to size if necessary and smooth any joins closed with your fingertips. If you are making a very long piece (e.g. to go all the way around the sides of a cake), lightly dust the surface with icing sugar, roll up the paste and position the end against the cake before unrolling it around the sides.

3 Allow to firm for several hours, as above.

TIP

Occasionally, especially when covering unusual cake shapes, you may find you have a stubborn pleat in the sugarpaste. It is often quicker to pinch it together and cut away the spare paste than to stretch it out and smooth it over. To remove the cut line, press the join closed by pinching gently then rub with your hands until the join is blended in. A little icing sugar on your fingers will help to remove the line completely.

COVERING A CAKE BOARD (DRUM)

1   Moisten the surface of the cake board slightly with a little cooled, boiled water using a pastry brush.

2   Knead the sugarpaste and roll out on a non-stick board dusted with icing sugar. Make sure the paste is big enough to cover the board and is no more than 2–3mm (just under $^1/_8$") thick. When rolling out, move the paste around to prevent sticking but do not turn it over.

3   Carefully fold the sugarpaste over the rolling pin, lift the sugarpaste and position it on the cake board. Gently smooth over the top of the covered cake board with a cake smoother.

4   Hold the board underneath with one hand and, using a plain-bladed knife, trim away the excess sugarpaste from around the edge. If you prefer a slightly rounded look, rub around the edge with a cake smoother until the paste becomes thin and tears away easily. Set aside to dry for at least 24 hours. You can always add 1tsp of CMC to the sugarpaste to help it firm up more quickly.

5   To finish the board, you will need to trim the edge with coordinating 15mm-width ribbon (this is slightly deeper than the cake board to allow for the depth of the sugarpaste covering). Measure the length needed to go around the board and allow an extra 2cm (¾") or so to overlap at the back.

6   Rub a non-toxic, solid glue stick around the cake board edge, taking care not to touch the sugarpaste covering. If you prefer, double-sided tape can be used instead. Starting at the back of the cake, stick the ribbon around the cake board edge, running your finger along the bottom to keep the ribbon straight. Overlap the ribbon slightly and cut off the excess at the join. Ensure the join is positioned at the back of the cake.

DOWELLING A CAKE

If a cake has two or more tiers or is particularly tall, you will need to dowel the lower tiers after they have been coated to make sure that the cakes stack evenly and are well-supported and balanced.

1   Make a template of the cake top from greaseproof paper and fold in half twice to find the centre. Draw a circle on the paper around the central point – the circle must fit within the size and shape of the tier that will be placed on top in order to support it. Mark the dowel points evenly around the circle – the number of dowels you need will depend on the size of the cake and number of tiers (see each project for details).

2   Using the template and a pointed tool (or the tip of a knife), mark the position of the dowels on the cake. Insert the dowels into the cake, ensuring that they are vertical and go all the way down to the cake board. Using a pencil, mark each dowel just above the level of the sugarpaste covering, making sure the pencil does not touch the sugarpaste itself. Alternatively, score each dowel carefully with a knife.

3   Remove the dowels, place them on a work surface and line up the bottom of each. The markings may vary, so find the lowest mark and score all the dowels at this point with a craft knife (this ensures the cake stands upright, has no gaps and does not lean). Snap each dowel to size (if using plastic dowels, otherwise cut to size) and then insert them back into the holes in the cake; they should each sit level with the cake top (or just below it if the cake is uneven).

Important note: Make sure the dowels and any other inedible items on the cake are removed before serving.

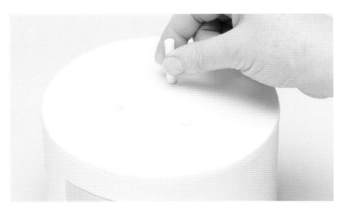

COVERING MINI CAKES WITH SUGARPASTE

Mini cakes are popular at any celebration, either alongside a larger cake or instead of one, and look extremely pretty and stylish when presented well. Suggested designs are given alongside each project which coordinate with the style of the main cake, so you can use these as inspiration or create your own designs.

Mini cakes can be made in several different shapes, including square and round. You can cut these from sheet cakes using good-quality, deep cutters, or I recommend using purpose-made mini cake bakeware and liners, available from sugarcraft stockists (see page 152). Silicone bakeware is useful for unusual shapes such as spheres and domes as the cakes can be turned out easily.

1 If required, cut one or two layers in the cake, depending on the size and shape. For ball shapes, sandwich the two halves together. Layer and crumb-coat the cake with filling (see recipes on pages 10 to 12).

2 Roll the sugarpaste a little thinner than you would for a large cake – around 2mm (under $1/8$") deep – then cover in the usual way (see page 20). Use a cake smoother to press the top and sides smooth.

3 Trim the paste neatly around the base of the cake. You can speed this up by using a hollow cutter the same shape and slightly larger than the mini cake to cut around the base cleanly and neatly. Simply move the cutter down over the mini cake, press it into the excess paste around the base then remove.

4 Place each mini cake on a small cake card or piece of greaseproof paper cut to size to protect and seal the cake and then decorate as required.

TIP

Mini cakes make great party bag fillers as an alternative to the traditional slice of cake. Decorate as required, then place in small boxes or cellophane bags tied with coordinating ribbon.

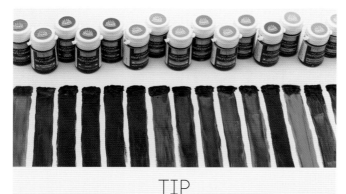

TIP

Paste food colours are concentrated, so only add a tiny amount of paste food colour at a time using a cocktail stick until the desired colour is achieved. Blend the colour into the paste by kneading well and allow to 'rest' in an airtight food-grade polythene bag for a couple of hours before use.

USING COLOUR

Food colourings are available as liquids, paints, pastes and dusts (also known as powders). Liquid colours and paints are generally used for painting onto sugar; pastes are ideal for colouring roll-out icings (such as sugarpaste and modelling paste) and royal icing; and dusts can be brushed onto the surface of sugar pieces or mixed with clear alcohol to make a quick-drying paint.

Squires Kitchen makes a huge range of colours for cake and food decoration. All of their colours are edible, light-fast, tartrazine-free and glycerine-free and are readily available from Squires Kitchen (see page 152) or your local stockist. If you are not using ready-coloured pastes and icings, you will need to colour them at least two hours before starting a project to allow the colour to develop.

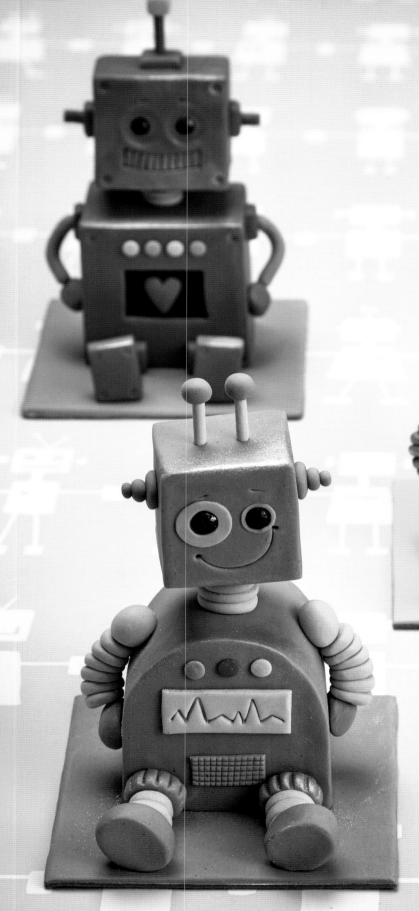

Projects

Stegosaurus

If you're hosting a prehistoric party, this smiling stegosaurus will make a fun and friendly centrepiece. I've used a polystyrene dummy for the bottom half of the dinosaur, but you can always make the whole body from cake if you need more servings.

EDIBLES

20cm (8") half-sphere or bowl-shaped cake, 4.5cm (1¾") deep (see recipes on pages 6–9)

20cm (8") round cake, 4.5cm (1¾") deep (see recipes on pages 6–9)

350g (12¼oz) cake filling (see recipes on pages 10–12)

200g (7oz) chocolate ganache or melted white chocolate (see page 12)

Edible glue (see page 14)

Dust (powder) food colour: vine green (SK)

Sugarpaste (rolled fondant):

    900g (2lb) pale green

    370g (13oz) pale orange

Modelling paste (see page 14):

    700g (1lb 8¾oz) green

    400g (14oz) pale orange

    30g (1oz) dark green

    Tiny piece of white and black

EQUIPMENT

Basic equipment (see pages 15–17)

20cm (8") half-sphere polystyrene dummy

35cm (14") round cake board

20cm (8") round cake card

10 paper lolly sticks

Food-safe cake dowel: 12cm (5") long

1.15m x 15mm width (46" x ⅝") satin ribbon: orange

Round cutter: 5cm (2")

CAKE BOARD

1 Cover the cake board with pale orange sugarpaste (see page 21). Set aside to dry.

CAKE

2 Level the top of the cakes and cut each of them into two layers. Assemble the layers with the domed cake on top of the round cake and trim down the sides with a serrated knife to make a neat dome shape. Sandwich the layers together with the cake filling of your choice and attach a cake card to the base of the cake.

3 Use a serrated knife to cut a small amount off the top of the half-sphere dummy to create a flat base. Do this in a separate room away from the cake and wipe away any polystyrene particles.

4 Place the cake onto the wider flat side of the half-sphere dummy. Spread a layer of ganache or melted chocolate over the surface of the cake and the join between the cake and the dummy. Keep the shape neat, mirroring the shape of the dummy underneath to make a ball.

5 Moisten the cake and dummy with a little cooled, boiled water or edible glue, ensuring the dummy is well covered so the sugarpaste will stick easily. Roll out the pale green sugarpaste and cover the cake completely, smoothing down and around the sphere (see page 20).

6 Use the tip of a knife to cut out a 4cm (1½") circle from the centre of the cake board covering, then remove the paste. Moisten the exposed board and the surrounding area with edible glue then place the cake on the cake board.

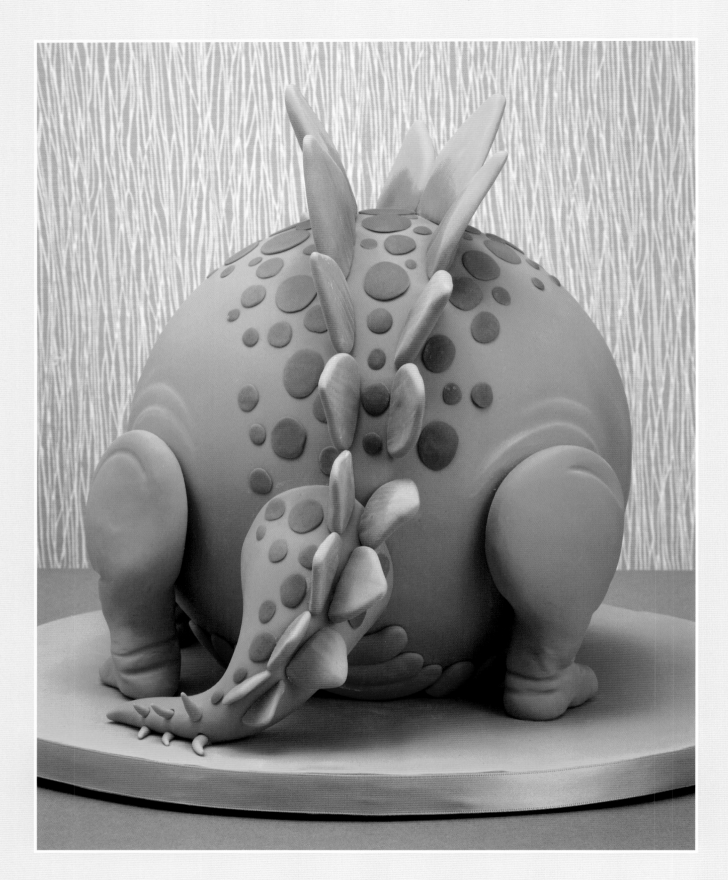

HEAD AND NECK

7 Push the cake dowel into one side of the polystyrene dummy where the head will be positioned, leaving around 5cm (2") of the dowel protruding. Roll 75g (2½oz) of green modelling paste into a rounded teardrop shape for the neck and cut both ends straight. Moisten the dowel and the surrounding area on the body then push the neck onto the dowel so it sits neatly following the contours of the round cake.

8 To make the head, roll 100g (3½oz) of green modelling paste into a ball. Roll the ball back and forth, pressing halfway down the paste to round off the muzzle. Push the paste up to make a deep indent between the head and the muzzle then roll the handle of a paintbrush over the surface to make another wrinkle. Smooth over and flatten the eye area.

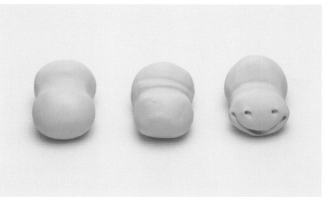

9 Push a round cutter into the bottom half of the muzzle to mark on the mouth and make dimples in the corners with the end of a paintbrush. Gently push the head onto the dowel so it sits up against the neck and is looking sideways, securing with edible glue. Push the end of a paintbrush into the muzzle and lift it up slightly to make the nostrils.

10 Model two flattened ovals of white modelling paste and secure them just above the muzzle. Add smaller ovals of black modelling paste on top and attach tiny white balls at the one o'clock position to make highlights. Roll a tiny ball of green modelling paste, press it down and cut in half to make two eyelids, securing over the top of each eye. Make two small eyebrows in the same way and attach towards the top of the head. Place the head aside to firm up.

TAIL

11 Roll 145g (5oz) of green modelling paste into a long, pointed teardrop shape. Flatten the larger, rounded end then stick it in position at the side of the cake. Smooth around the join so it sits neatly against the body and curl the tip of the tail around to the front.

SCALES

12 Roll several sausages in graduating sizes from 60g (2oz) of orange modelling paste. Press down on each sausage with a cake smoother and stick in place, working from the underside of the neck down onto the tummy. Cut the scales for the middle of the tummy in half then smooth them in place on either side of the cake so they look as if they continue underneath.

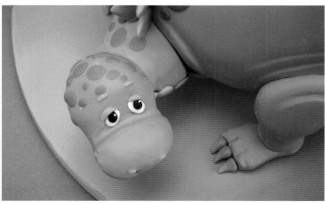

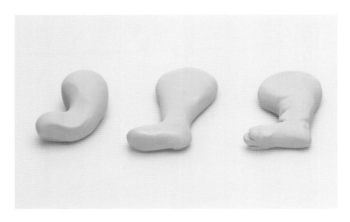

LEGS

13 Use 75g (2½oz) of green modelling paste for each front leg and split the remaining green paste in half for the back legs. To make each of the legs, roll the paste into a ball then roll it back and forth, pressing on the centre. Push the paste down towards one end to round off the foot. Press down on the foot and pinch either side to lengthen and narrow it. Make cuts in the foot for the toes, then slice the end of the toes flat. Roll a paintbrush handle over the surface to create folds in the skin then press down on the opposite end to flatten and widen the top of the leg. Stick in position on the side of the cake as you finish each one, smoothing over the join and following the contour of the rounded body. Mark a couple of creases above the legs with the handle of a paintbrush.

14 For the claws, roll teardrop shapes from pea-sized amounts of orange modelling paste. Moisten with edible glue then press gently but firmly against the ends of the toes. Curl the tip of each claw under slightly.

BACK SPIKES (PLATES)

15 To make the largest spike, roll 25g (just over ¾oz) of orange modelling paste into a teardrop shape and press flat with a cake smoother. Smooth around the outside edge so the centre of the spike is slightly thicker. Moisten a lolly stick with edible glue then push it into the wide end halfway up the spike. Roll a paintbrush handle over the surface to create ripples then set aside to dry. Repeat to make a second spike the same size.

16 Make each of the smallest plates from 2g (pinch) of orange modelling paste, but do not dowel them.

17 Use the remaining orange modelling paste to make 11 more pairs of spikes that graduate in size between the largest and smallest spikes. Support the eight largest ones with lolly sticks.

18 Gently insert the largest pair of spikes into the centre of the stegosaurus' back, so they sit a few centimetres apart. Insert the remaining spikes in front and behind the largest pair, so they get smaller towards the tail and the head. Attach the smaller spikes with edible glue. Use any leftover orange modelling paste to make six very small, pointed teardrops and attach them in pairs at the end of the tail.

19 Roll several ovals and balls from the dark green modelling paste and press each of them flat with a cake smoother. Stick them over the stegosaurus' back, head and tail so they graduate in size, smoothing each gently onto the surface of the cake with your finger.

20 Mix the green dust food colour with a sprinkle of icing sugar, then brush this over the back spikes using a dry paintbrush. (The icing sugar will help prevent the colour from going patchy as you brush it on.) Add more at the very base of each spike to intensify the colour.

21 To finish the cake, trim the edge of the cake board with orange ribbon (see page 21) and set aside to dry.

Mini Dinosaur Friends

EDIBLES
(per cake)

2 x 7cm (2¾") half-sphere cakes (see recipes on pages 6–9)

30g (1oz) cake filling (see recipes on pages 10–12)

Edible glue (see page 14)

Tyrannosaurus Rex

Sugarpaste (rolled fondant):
   60g (2oz) pale orange
   30g (1oz) green

Modelling paste (see page 14):
   90g (3oz) pale orange
   A little dark orange, white and black

Triceratops

Sugarpaste (rolled fondant):
   60g (2oz) lime green
   30g (1oz) orange

Modelling paste (see page 14):
   90g (3oz) lime green
   5g (just under ¼oz) orange
   A little bright green, white and black

Diplodocus

Sugarpaste (rolled fondant):
   60g (2oz) blue
   30g (1oz) green

Modelling paste (see page 14):
   65g (2¼oz) blue
   A little white and black

EQUIPMENT
(per cake)

Basic equipment (see pages 15–17)

10cm (4") round cake card

Round cutter: 5cm (2")

A lolly stick

1   Cover the cake card with 30g (1oz) of green or orange sugarpaste. Press a rolling pin over the surface to add texture and set aside.

2   Sandwich the two half-sphere cakes together with a little cake filling, then spread more cake filling over the surface of the cake. Cover the cake completely with 60g (2oz) of sugarpaste in the colour of your chosen dinosaur, smoothing down and around the sphere. Gently roll the cake on a work surface to smooth the sugarpaste and stick in position on a cake card. Mark lines down the back with a paintbrush handle.

TYRANNOSAURUS REX

3   Roll 15g (½oz) of pale orange modelling paste into a rounded teardrop for the neck. Push the fuller end against the body and use a little edible glue to secure. Moisten a lolly stick with edible glue and push it down through the neck and into the body, leaving a little protruding for the head. Mark wrinkles on the neck with the end of a paintbrush.

4   Use 20g (¾oz) of orange modelling paste to make a smaller version of the stegosaurus head on the main cake, but cut deeper into the mouth to open it up. Stick the head in position then add

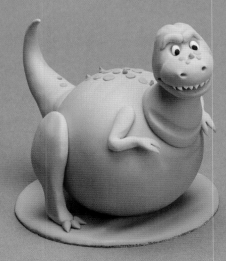

Tyrannosaurus Rex   Triceratops   Diplodocus

tiny, white teardrop shapes for the teeth. Make thicker, arched eyebrows to give a scary expression.

5 Use 15g (½oz) of orange modelling paste to make a pointed teardrop for the tail and attach it so it curls upwards. Split 5g (¼oz) of orange modelling paste in half for the two tiny front legs. Roll each piece to 4cm (1½") long and round off each end. Make a cut in the ends and gently pinch to create the claws. Bend the legs halfway and stick in position with the claws turned out slightly.

6 Split 30g (1oz) of orange modelling paste into two pieces for the back legs. Shape them as for the main cake, but make the legs longer and the feet smaller. Cut across each foot and add three small, teardrop-shaped claws. Stick tiny horns and flattened circles of dark orange modelling paste over the back and face, sticking one horn to the centre of the muzzle.

TRICERATOPS

7 Roll 45g (1½oz) of lime green modelling paste into a ball for the head. Roll the ball back and forth in the centre to round off the ends and create a dip for the eye area. Pinch up the paste to make a heart-shaped fan around the back of the head. Stroke the handle of a paintbrush over the surface to indent lines. Make the mouth with a round cutter and indent eye sockets with a ball tool. Push the end of a paintbrush into the muzzle to create nostrils. Make the eyes and eyelids as for the main cake.

TIP

If the tail is too soft to stay in place, either support it with some kitchen paper until dry or insert a lolly stick through the paste.

10 To make the pale orange coral, make several long teardrops from pale orange sugarpaste then make a hole in the end of each piece with the handle of a paintbrush. Wind the handle around to widen the hole, then position the pieces of coral in a group at the base of the cake and secure.

11 To make the pink anemone fans, roll small teardrop shapes from the dark pink sugarpaste and press down to flatten each one. Use scissors to cut along the fuller end to make fan shapes and arrange them around the cake. For the rounded pink sea anemones, roll pieces of dark pink sugarpaste into balls. Pinch the paste a third of the way from the end to bring out a cone shape then push a small ball tool into the end to make a hole. Flatten out the paste around the edge of the hole and snip into it with a pair of scissors to make several fronds.

12 To make the seaweed, roll long sausages of green sugarpaste and flatten them down with a cake smoother. Push a paintbrush handle into the sides to bring out the fronds, then smooth over and round them off. Stick around the sides of the base tier.

13 For the dark orange flowers, roll large pea-sized amounts of dark orange sugarpaste and flatten them down. Roll a paintbrush handle around the edge of each piece to thin out and frill the paste. Secure up the sides of the base tier with a little edible glue.

14 To make the shoal of fish, roll tiny teardrops from yellow sugarpaste then roll a paintbrush handle over the end of each piece to flatten the tail. Make a small indent for the eye using the tip of a cocktail stick. Attach across the front of the top-tier cake with a little edible glue.

15 For the starfish, roll out some more yellow sugarpaste and cut out a star shape with a large calyx cutter. Pinch up the centre of the paste, turn up the very tips of the arms and secure to the cake board.

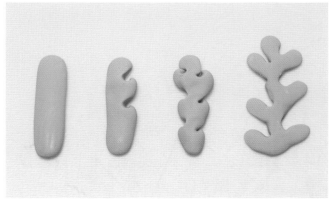

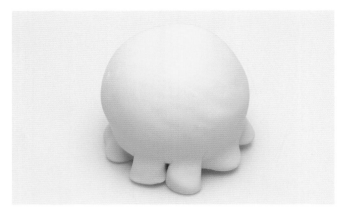

FISH

16 Roll out 65g (2¼oz) of yellow sugarpaste and cover one of the marshmallow rice cereal balls, smoothing down and around the shape. Pinch out the excess sugarpaste at the back to make the tail. Pinch the base of the tail to narrow it, then flatten and widen the end. Indent the mouth using a 2.5cm (1") round cutter and add dimples in the corners with the end of a paintbrush. Push the paintbrush handle into the bottom lip to shape the mouth.

17 Use some yellow sugarpaste to model a small triangle for the dorsal fin and two flattened teardrops for the pectoral fins on the sides. Roll out thin strips of pale orange and black sugarpaste and attach them across the back of the fish.

18 Indent the eye sockets with a bone or ball tool, then add two flattened ovals of white sugarpaste for the eyes. Make two smaller flattened ovals from black sugarpaste and secure on top. Model two tiny strips of black paste for the eyelashes and add a tiny white ball on each eye at the one o'clock position. Push the fish down onto the central dowel at the top of the cake and secure at the base with a little edible glue.

19 Make the pink fish in the same way using 65g (2¼oz) of pink sugarpaste to cover the marshmallow rice cereal body. Make a large patch of purple sugarpaste and secure it over the back of the fish. For the dorsal fin, roll a long flattened teardrop from purple sugarpaste and cut the end straight. Insert the shorter dowel into the top of the base tier and push the side of the pink fish onto it. Dust the fish with bright yellow dust food colour.

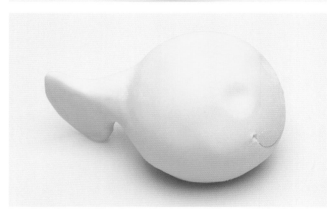

CRAB

20 Roll two thirds of the remaining dark orange sugarpaste into an oval shape. Indent the mouth with a round cutter, add dimples with the handle of a paintbrush and stick in place on the blue coral. Model two ovals from the dark orange sugarpaste and stick them on top of the crab's head for the eyes. Secure a flattened white oval, a smaller black oval and a tiny ball of white paste onto each eye.

21 For the claws, roll two long, thin sausages and round off each end. Press down on the ends and cut out a small V-shape from each one using a pair of fine scissors. Bend each arm halfway and pinch out at the elbow. Stick in place so one arm is waving, supported by the green coral.

TURTLE

22 Roll 45g (1½oz) of green sugarpaste into a ball and press down on it to flatten it slightly. Roll a 10g (¼oz) ball of green sugarpaste, flatten it and secure it under the front to lift up the body.

23 For the head, roll 30g (1oz) of green sugarpaste into a ball then roll it back and forth at one end to round off the head and bring out a neck. Indent two eye sockets using a bone or ball tool and add two small balls of black paste for the eyes. Indent the mouth as for the yellow fish. For the eyebrows, roll two large pea-sized teardrop shapes from some more green sugarpaste and stick in place on top of the head with a little edible glue, smoothing the pointed ends into the surface.

24 To make the flippers, split the remaining green sugarpaste into four equal pieces and roll them into long teardrop shapes. Press down on each piece with a cake smoother. Stick in position then decorate with different-sized spots of dark green sugarpaste.

25 For the shell, roll 45g (1½oz) of dark green sugarpaste into a ball and press down on it to make a dome shape. Press the large, round cutter around the outside edge. Decorate with green spots in the same way as the flippers.

TIP

I made an indent in the shell with the rounded edge of my cutter, but if you only have a straight edge then smooth the paste over with your fingers to soften the line.

BLUE WHALE

26 Moisten the surface of the small sphere cake with a little cooled, water or edible glue. Roll out the remaining dark blue sugarpaste and cover as for the yellow fish. Use a large, round cutter to indent a wide, smiling mouth low on the face and add dimples with the end of a paintbrush. Make eye sockets and eyes as for the yellow fish. Smooth your fingertip from the underside of each eye to the corners of the mouth to round off the cheeks. Decorate the whale's back with different-sized spots of light blue sugarpaste and make an indent in the top for the blowhole.

27 Trim the edge of the cake board with aqua blue ribbon to finish (see page 21).

Killer Whale and Dolphin Mini Cakes

EDIBLES
(per cake)

2 x 7cm (2¾") half-sphere (see recipes on pages 6–9)

30g (1oz) cake filling (see recipes on pages 10–12)

Sugarpaste (rolled fondant):

Killer whale

60g (2oz) black

30g (1oz) pale blue

30g (1oz) white

Dolphin

90g (3oz) grey

30g (1oz) light blue

A little white and black

EQUIPMENT
(per cake)

Basic equipment (see pages 15–17)

10cm (4") round cake card

Round cutter: 2cm (¾")

1 Cover the cake card with approximately 30g (1oz) of light blue sugarpaste.

2 Sandwich the half-sphere cakes together with a little cake filling, then spread the remaining filling over the cake. Moisten the surface with a little cooled, boiled water or edible glue.

KILLER WHALE

3 Attach a 5g (just under ¼oz) sausage of black sugarpaste to the front of the cake to pad out the nose area. Roll out some white sugarpaste and use it to cover the bottom half of the cake. Use black sugarpaste to cover the top half and the nose area in one go. Pinch out the tail from the black sugarpaste at the back of the cake and cut it to shape with scissors. Make the fins from black sugarpaste in the same way as for the yellow fish on the main cake.

4 Use a 2cm (¾") round cutter to cut out the patches around the eyes. Smooth over each opening to round them off then fill with pieces of white sugarpaste. Make the eyes in the same way as for the yellow fish on the main cake.

DOLPHIN

5 Pad out the nose with a 15g (½oz) ball of grey sugarpaste. Roll out the remaining grey sugarpaste and cover the cake completely, smoothing down and around the shape. Pinch out and shape the tail in the same way as for the killer whale. Make the fins from grey sugarpaste in the same way as for the yellow fish on the main cake.

6 Roll the side of a paintbrush handle across the bottom of the nose to open up the mouth and smooth it over with your fingers. Make the eyes and eyelashes in the same way as for the yellow fish on the main cake.

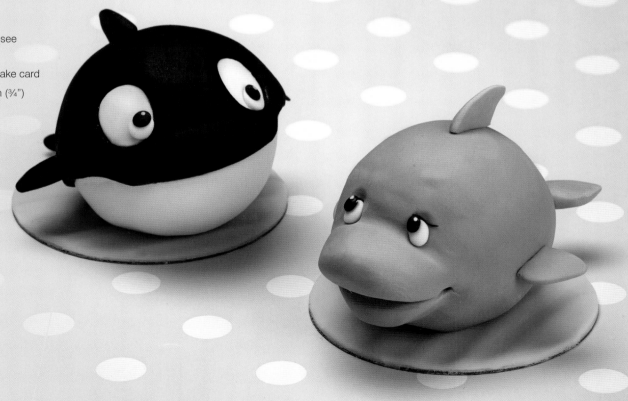

Monster Truck

My grandson is obsessed with cars and trucks, so I wanted to include a fun truck design when thinking of initial ideas for the book. This cake serves 15-20 people but if you need more servings then you could always make more cakes to look like rocks and arrange them on the party table.

EDIBLES

15cm (6") half-sphere or bowl-shaped cake, 8cm (3") deep (see recipes on pages 6–9)

20cm (8") square cake, 4cm (1½") deep (see recipes on pages 6–9)

2 x 7cm (2¾") half-sphere cakes, 4cm (1½") deep (see recipes on pages 6–9)

350g (12¼oz) cake filling (see recipes on pages 10–12)

300g (10½oz) marshmallow rice cereal (see page 11)

200g (7oz) chocolate ganache or melted white chocolate (see page 12)

Edible glue (see page 14)

Paste food colour: white (SK)

Sugarpaste (rolled fondant):

  1kg (2lb 3¼oz) beige

  580g (1lb 4½oz) red

  460g (1lb ¼oz) black

  25g (just over ¾oz) skin tone

Modelling paste (see page 14):

  75g (2½oz) blue

  45g (1½oz) black

  10g (¼oz) grey

  10g (¼oz) white

  5g (just under ¼oz) brown

  5g (just under ¼oz) skin tone

EQUIPMENT

Basic equipment (see pages 15–17)

30cm (12") round cake board

20cm x 10cm (8" x 4") rectangular cake card, cut to shape (see template on page 147)

7 food-safe cake dowels: 5 x 10cm (4") and 2 x 15cm (6") long

Round cutters: 3cm, 4cm and 5cm (1⅛", 1½" and 2")

1m x 15mm width (40" x ⅝") ribbon: chequered pattern

MARSHMALLOW RICE CEREAL HEAD AND WHEELS

1 Roll 15g (½oz) of marshmallow rice cereal into a ball for the head, rolling it over the work surface to smooth and shape it. Roll back and forth on one side to flatten the facial area slightly.

2 Split the remaining marshmallow rice cereal into four equally sized pieces for the wheels. Shape each piece into an 8cm (3") circle that is 4cm (1½") deep. Set aside.

CAKE BOARD

3 Cover the cake board with 285g (10oz) of beige sugarpaste (see page 21). Smooth the surface with a cake smoother then press a rolling pin over the board to create ripples and set aside to dry.

CAKES

4 Trim the crusts from the half-sphere cakes. Level only the very top of the largest half-sphere cake to keep the rounded shape, then cut it into two or three layers. Level the top of the two smaller half-sphere cakes completely and cut each one into two layers. Sandwich the cakes back together with cake filling, then spread a layer of cake filling over the surface of each one and leave to firm.

5 Roll out 350g (12¼oz) of beige sugarpaste and cover the large half-sphere cake completely, smoothing down and around the shape. Trim the excess from around the base and smooth the edge

to round it off. Smooth the side of your hand over small areas of the cake to create dents and make it look more rock-shaped. Spread some ganache or melted white chocolate over the underside of the cake and place it centrally on the cake board.

6 Cover the two smaller half-sphere cakes in the same way using 65g (2¼oz) of beige sugarpaste for each one. Place one at the back of the board and the other at the front to the right to help support the wheel later.

7 Shape the remaining beige sugarpaste into different-sized rocks and stick these randomly over the cake board, adding a larger one at the front to help support the front right wheel. Dowel the centre of the main cake with four 10cm (4") long dowels (see page 21) to support the truck.

8 Trim the crust from the square cake and level the top. Place the cake card template on top of the cake and cut the cake to shape. Remove the template and trim down the front of the cake at an angle, so it slopes down slightly. Round off the bonnet area then trim the sides of the cake at a slight angle.

9 Cut an 8cm x 6.5cm (3⅛" x 2½") piece from the cake trimmings and trim it to 2cm (¾") deep. Position it on top of the larger cake to make the cabin, then trim down the sides at a slight angle. Cut the larger cake into two layers and assemble them on the shaped cake card. Sandwich the layers together with cake filling, securing the cabin on top. Spread a layer of ganache or melted white chocolate over the surface (see page 19).

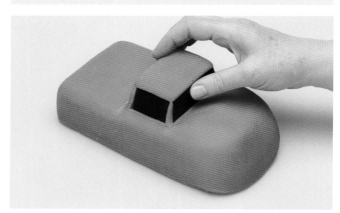

10 Roll out 370g (13oz) of red sugarpaste and cover the truck, smoothing down and around the shape. Trim any excess from around the base. Press two cake smoothers against the sides of the truck and on top of the cabin to straighten and smooth the sugarpaste. Run the edge of a cake smoother along the top of the cabin to bring out the roof. Cut away rectangles from the front and sides of the cabin to make the windows. Roll out some black sugarpaste very thinly, cut out three windows and stick these in the gaps. Make an indent down either side of the truck to define the doors and add a small oval handle to each one.

WHEELS

11 Roll out 100g (3½oz) of black sugarpaste and cover one of the marshmallow rice cereal wheels, smoothing around the shape with your hands. Cut away any excess paste from the underside and smooth over the join with a little edible glue to close it. Press a cake smoother over the surface to flatten it. Cut out a 3cm (1⅛") circle from the centre of the wheel and remove the sugarpaste. Roll the circle of paste out thinly, cut it into a 3cm (1⅛") circle using the same cutter

and replace it, smoothing over the join if necessary. Indent another circle just outside it with a 4cm (1½") round cutter to make the rim. Cover the remaining three wheels in the same way.

12 Split 20g (¾oz) of black sugarpaste into four equal pieces and roll them into balls. Stick one to the back of each wheel and press down with a cake smoother to flatten it. Use the end of a paintbrush to make a hole in the centre of each piece.

13 Roll out the blue modelling paste into a thin sheet and cut out four circles using a 3cm (1⅛") cutter. Stick one to the centre of each wheel then mark lines around the edge using the back of a knife. Roll out some black modelling paste into a thin sheet and cut out several short strips for the tyre treads, then attach them in pairs around the edge of each wheel. Attach two small, flattened circles of black modelling paste to the centre for the wheel nuts.

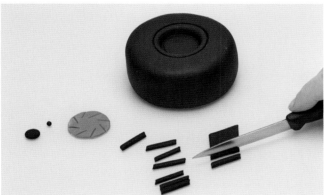

14 Roll 15g (½oz) of black sugarpaste into a 10cm (4") long sausage and flatten it with a rolling pin. Moisten one of the 15cm (6") long dowels with edible glue and wrap the paste around it, gently smoothing over the join and leaving the ends uncovered. Cover the second 15cm (6") dowel in the same way. Position the truck on the top of the main cake so it is tilted forward then slip the covered dowels under the truck. Push the back of each wheel onto the ends of the dowels and secure with edible glue.

DETAILING ON TRUCK

15 Divide 160g (5½oz) of red sugarpaste into four equal pieces then roll them into long teardrop shapes for the wheel arches. Curve them around the top of each wheel and secure in place. Roll another small teardrop of red sugarpaste, cut the end straight and attach to the centre of the bonnet. Roll two 10cm (4") long sausages from 25g (just over ¾oz) of red sugarpaste and stick them across the front and back of the cake to make the bumpers.

16 Make two flattened ovals of white modelling paste and two smaller ones from black modelling paste. Attach one of each to the front of the wheel arches to make the eyes and add two small teardrops of red sugarpaste for the eyebrows. Model seven smaller, flattened teardrops from the white modelling paste and stick them across the front bumper to make teeth. Roll five thin sausages of equal size from grey modelling paste and secure them to the front of the truck for the grille.

17 Cover a 10cm (4") dowel with red sugarpaste as explained in step 14, this time leaving 2cm (¾") exposed at the end, and set aside. Roll out some blue modelling paste into a thin sheet, cut out a 9.5cm x 11.5cm (3¾" x 4½") rectangle and secure over the top of the truck and back of the cabin. Push the red dowel down into the back of the truck and top with a tiny, flattened ball of red sugarpaste.

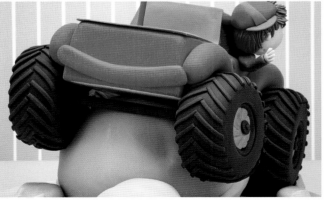

DRIVER

18 Model a small triangle of blue modelling paste and stick it in the bottom left-hand corner of the windscreen to make the driver's left shoulder. Roll 10g (¼oz) of blue modelling paste into a teardrop, roll out the narrow end to lengthen the sleeve and make an indent in the end with a paintbrush handle. Press in halfway along the arm to make it bend at the elbow then stick the paste in position at the side of the cabin. Place a little scrunched-up kitchen paper under the arm to support it whilst it dries.

19 Roll out the skin-tone sugarpaste and cover the marshmallow rice cereal ball for the head, smoothing around the shape and trimming any excess paste from the back. Rub the surface with a small ball of sugarpaste trimmings to create a smooth finish. Use a CelStick or veiner to indent the mouth, adding dimples in the corners. Smooth just underneath the mouth to bring out the chin and indent two eye sockets with your fingertips. Push a 10cm (4") dowel down through the body and into the cake then push the head onto it, securing at the base with a little edible glue.

20 Roll a tiny oval for the nose and two small balls for the ears from some skin-tone modelling paste. Make an indent in the centre of each ear with the end of a paintbrush and stick the ears and nose in place. Roll two tiny ovals of black modelling paste, secure them in the eye sockets and add a tiny highlight at the one o'clock position with white paste food colour.

21 Cut tiny strips of hair from the brown modelling paste and arrange them around the front of the head, leaving the top uncovered. For the hat, cut out a 5cm (2") circle of red sugarpaste and secure to the top of the driver's head, smoothing around the edge. Add a small peak and a central stripe from a little blue modelling paste.

22 For the driver's hand, roll a small ball of skin-tone modelling paste into a teardrop shape and press down to flatten it slightly. Make a cut for the thumb in the right-hand side then cut into the end to separate the fingers. Gently roll out each finger to lengthen and round it off. Roll the paste at the wrist, insert it into the end of the sleeve in a waving position and secure with edible glue.

FINISHING TOUCHES

23 Cut out a small triangle for the flag from a piece of rolled-out white modelling paste. Wrap the straight end around the pole and secure with edible glue. Add tiny squares of black modelling paste to make the chequered effect.

24 Trim the edge of the cake board with chequered ribbon to finish (see page 21).

Monster Truck Cupcakes

EDIBLES
(per cupcake)

Cupcake baked in a chequered paper case (see recipes on pages 6–9)

30g (1oz) cake filling (see recipes on pages 10–12)

Sugarpaste (rolled fondant):

20g (¾oz) beige

Modelling paste (see page 14):

15g (½oz) chassis colour

10g (¼oz) black

A little of a contrasting colour

Liquid food colour: black diluted with a little cooled, boiled water (SK)

EQUIPMENT
(per cupcake)

Basic equipment (see pages 15–17)

Small piece of thin cake card

Round cutter: 8cm (3¹/₈")

1 Bake as many cupcakes as required and spread cake filling over the top of each one. Cut out an 8cm (3¹/₈") circle from the beige sugarpaste and place over the top of the cupcake. Add some small rocks from the beige sugarpaste trimmings.

2 Split the black modelling paste into four equal pieces and shape into wheels, flattening each piece slightly. Indent the centre with the end of a paintbrush and add a small circle of the contrasting colour and a tiny ball of black modelling paste.

3 For the chassis, roll 10g (¼oz) of your chosen modelling paste into a short sausage. Press the side of a knife into one end at an angle to shape the bonnet and press down at the back. Cut small pieces of thin cake card into shape for the windows, push into the paste then remove. Paint the windows with a little diluted black food colour.

4 Stick the wheels to the chassis with a little edible glue. Make and attach smaller versions of the bumpers and wheel arches following the instructions for the main cake. Stick a thin rectangle of modelling paste in a contrasting colour over the back of the truck. Position the truck on top of the cupcake.

Puppy Love

This cute puppy cake and its accompanying mini cakes were inspired by the Springer Spaniels that are part of our family – Bella, Choccy, Daisy and Lucky. A great cake for little animal lovers, you can always adapt this design to look like your own family pet.

EDIBLES

2 x 15cm (6") half-sphere or bowl-shaped cakes (see recipes on pages 6–9)

4 x 7cm (2¾") half-sphere or bowl-shaped cakes (see recipes on pages 6–9)

350g (12¼oz) cake filling (see recipes on pages 10–12)

200g (7oz) chocolate ganache or melted white chocolate (see page 12)

400g (14oz) marshmallow rice cereal (see page 11)

Edible glue (see page 14)

Lustre dust (powder) food colour: silver (SK)

A few drops of lemon extract (or clear alcohol, e.g. gin or vodka)

Dust (powder) food colours: golden brown and red (SK)

Paste food colour: white (SK)

Sugarpaste (rolled fondant):
    1.4kg (3lb 1½oz) ivory
    315g (11oz) red
    260g (9oz) chocolate brown

Modelling paste (see page 14):
    30g (1oz) black
    25g (just over ¾oz) red

EQUIPMENT

Basic equipment (see pages 15–17)

30cm (12") round cake board

3 food-safe cake dowels: 20cm (8") long

Round cutter: 5cm (2")

CelStick (optional)

1m x 15mm width (40" x ⅝") ribbon: red gingham

CAKE BOARD

1 Cover the cake board with red sugarpaste (see page 21) and set aside to dry.

MARSHMALLOW RICE CEREAL HEAD AND FRONT LEGS

2 Roll 225g (8oz) of marshmallow rice cereal into a ball for the head and squeeze the top to narrow it slightly. Model 25g (just over ¾oz) of the mix into an oval shape for the muzzle and stick it to the front of the head. Split 20g (¾oz) of the mixture in half and use it to pad out the cheeks.

3 Split the remaining marshmallow rice cereal in two for the front legs. Squeeze the centre of each piece to narrow it slightly and round off the end, making the paws slightly larger. Make the raised paw fuller at the top, but smooth over the top of the other paw to flatten it down. Set aside.

TIP

If the marshmallow mixture is sticky, leave it to cool down a little more. If it's still too sticky to handle, rub a little butter or oil onto your hands.

CAKES

4 Level the top of the two 15cm (6") half-sphere cakes, cut each cake into two layers and sandwich them back together with cake filling. Sandwich the two half-sphere cakes together to make a ball, then spread a layer of ganache or melted white chocolate over the surface as a crumb coat. Position the cake centrally on the cake board.

5 Stick the smaller half-spheres together with cake filling to make two balls for the back feet and press them down to flatten slightly. Spread a layer of ganache or melted white chocolate over the surface of the cakes then place them either side of the main cake. Position one cake flat and one upright, securing with a dab of ganache or chocolate.

BACK LEGS

6 Split 60g (2oz) of ivory sugarpaste in half and roll into two balls. Press each ball into the space between the back feet and the body to make the top of the legs, smoothing the paste onto the surface of the cake and feet to secure them in place.

NECK

7 Roll a 60g (2oz) ball of ivory sugarpaste and place it on top of the body. Smooth the paste around the bottom of the neck onto the surface of the cake.

COVERING THE CAKE

8 Roll out 800g (1lb 12oz) of ivory sugarpaste and cover the cake completely, smoothing down and around the shape (see page 20). Trim any excess paste from around the base. Roll out some of the ivory sugarpaste trimmings into a thin sheet, cut out a 5cm (2") circle with the cutter and position it over the upright back paw.

9 Stroke the paste with a CelStick or the handle of a paintbrush to create the fur texture. Once you have finished texturing the paste, push a dowel down through the body until it touches the cake board and secure at the neck with a little edible glue.

FRONT LEGS

10 Cover the front legs with 90g (3oz) of ivory sugarpaste and texture as before. Push a dowel down into the top of the raised front leg then push the exposed dowel into the front of the cake at an angle, securing at the join with a little edible glue. Position the other leg against the front of the body, smoothing the join closed with a little edible glue. Use the back of a knife to make three marks in the end of each paw.

HEAD

11 Roll out the remaining ivory sugarpaste and cover the head completely, smoothing around the shape and tucking the excess paste underneath. Smooth around the muzzle and cheeks to give them more definition and indent two eye sockets with your fingertips.

12 Using a CelStick or a paintbrush handle, stroke the paste upwards at the front of the muzzle to make a central line. Following the muzzle line, push into the cheeks to make the corners of the mouth. Texture the fur as before then use scissors to make tufts of hair by snipping into the paste on the head, forehead and cheeks.

13 Push the head onto the dowel in the body so it is very slightly tilted, then secure at the base with a little edible glue. Blend in the paste at the neck to disguise the join.

EARS

14 Cut the remaining dowel in half to use as supports for the ears. Split 100g (3½oz) of brown modelling paste in half and roll each piece into a sausage that tapers at both ends. Moisten the dowels with edible glue then push one into each ear. Pinch the paste around the edge to create a fur effect then push them into the top of the head, securing with a little edible glue. Roll the ends of the ears between your fingers so the fur flicks up and texture as before.

TAIL

15 Roll 90g (3oz) of brown sugarpaste into a thick, tapering sausage and texture as before. Stick in position up the back of the cake, turning the end out a little at the top.

PATCHES AND PAW PAD

16 Roll out thin circles of brown sugarpaste and stick them over the surface of the cake. Texture as before and blend the edges of the paste. Make four small, brown circles and one larger brown circle and stick them onto the upright back paw.

EYES AND NOSE

17 Roll two oval eyes from black modelling paste and stick them in place above the muzzle. Add a tiny dot of white paste food colour on each eye at the one o'clock position.

18 Set aside 5g (just under ¼oz) of black modelling paste for the bone on the collar then roll the remainder into a ball for the nose. Pinch the base of the ball to narrow it slightly, then attach to the muzzle. Mix red dust food colour with a sprinkle of icing sugar and brush over the cheeks. Add a little icing sugar to the brown dust food colour and brush over the cake, adding more colour around the base of the neck.

COLLAR

19 Roll out the red modelling paste into a thin sheet then cut a 25cm x 1.5cm (10" x ⅝") strip for the collar. Wrap it around the dog's neck then close the join at the front with a little sausage of red paste.

20 To make the bone, roll the remaining black modelling paste into a sausage shape then press into the centre to round off the ends. Press the back of a knife into each end then paint with silver lustre dust mixed with lemon extract (or clear alcohol). Stick the bone to the cake so it is just touching the collar.

21 Trim the edge of the cake board with red gingham ribbon to finish (see page 21).

Mini Playful Puppies

EDIBLES
(per cake)

2 x 7cm (2¾") half-sphere cakes (see recipes on pages 6–9)

30g (1oz) cake filling (see recipes on pages 10–12)

20g (¾oz) chocolate ganache or melted white chocolate (see pages 10–12)

60g (2oz) marshmallow rice cereal (see page 11)

Sugarpaste (rolled fondant):

    225g (½lb) brown, ivory or a mixture of both

    A little black, red and white

EQUIPMENT
(per cake)

Basic equipment (see pages 15–17)

Lolly sticks for ears, neck and legs (dependent on pose)

Cake card (optional)

Small heart cutter

1 Sandwich two half-sphere cakes together with a little cake filling. Use a little ganache or melted white chocolate (or a little sugarpaste) to build up the neck area so the body is teardrop-shaped. Spread a layer of cake filling over the surface of the cake to seal in the crumbs.

2 Make the head from 35g (1¼oz) of marshmallow rice cereal, then add a muzzle and cheeks in the same way as for the main puppy project. Split 20g (¾oz) of marshmallow rice cereal in half and shape into balls for the back paws.

3 Cover the cakes with either brown or ivory sugarpaste and texture the cakes in the same way as for the main cake. Model the ears, tail and front legs from sugarpaste and insert lolly sticks into the ears and legs to make them stand up.

4 Use black sugarpaste to make the facial features, following the instructions for the main cake. Make a strip of white sugarpaste for the collar and cut out a heart from red sugarpaste for the tag. Add patches of brown or ivory sugarpaste and texture in the same way as before.

Alien Encounter

This big, green planet cake, complete with friendly aliens, is perfect if you want to make a centrepiece that is out of this world. Half of the planet is made from cake and the other half is made from a polystyrene dummy, but you could make both halves from cake if you need more servings.

EDIBLES

20cm (8") half-sphere or bowl-shaped cake, 4.5cm (1¾") deep (see recipes on pages 6–9)

20cm (8") round cake, 4.5cm (1¾") deep (see recipes on pages 6–9)

350g (12¼oz) cake filling (see recipes on pages 10–12)

200g (7oz) chocolate ganache or melted white chocolate (see page 12)

50g (1¾oz) marshmallow rice cereal (see page 11)

Edible glue (see page 14)

Paste food colour: red (SK)

Dust (powder) food colour: bright yellow (SK)

Lustre dust (powder) food colour: silver (SK)

A few drops of lemon extract (or clear alcohol, e.g. gin or vodka)

Sugarpaste (rolled fondant):
    1.14kg (2½lb) light green
    370g (13oz) navy blue
    65g (2¼oz) red

Modelling paste (see page 14):
    65g (2¼oz) green
    65g (2¼oz) red
    15g (½oz) orange
    10g (¼oz) black
    10g (¼oz) dark mauve
    10g (¼oz) mauve
    10g (¼oz) white
    10g (¼oz) yellow
    2g (pinch) pale blue

EQUIPMENT

Basic equipment (see pages 15–17)

20cm (8") half-sphere polystyrene dummy

20cm (8") round cake card

35cm (14") round cake board

1.15m x 15mm width (46" x ⅝") satin ribbon: navy blue

Round cutters: 2cm, 2.5cm, 3cm, 3.5cm, 4cm, 5.5cm, 8cm and 10cm (¾", 1", 1¼", 1⅜", 1½", 2¼", 3" and 4")

Food-safe cake dowel: 12–15cm (5–6") long

3 small paper lolly sticks

MARSHMALLOW RICE CEREAL ROCKET

1 Roll the marshmallow rice cereal mixture into a long egg shape and press down on the work surface to flatten the base. Set aside for later.

CAKE AND CAKE BOARD

2 Cover the cake board with navy blue sugarpaste (see page 21) and set aside.

3 Level the top of the cakes and cut each of them into two layers. Assemble the layers with the domed cake on top of the round cake and trim down the sides with a serrated knife to make a neat dome shape. Sandwich the layers together with the cake filling of your choice and attach a cake card to the base of the cake.

4 Use a serrated knife to cut a small amount off the top of the half-sphere dummy to create a flat base. Do this in a separate room away from the cake and wipe away any polystyrene particles.

5 Place the cake onto the wider flat side of the half-sphere dummy. Spread a layer of ganache or melted chocolate over the surface of the cake and the join between the cake and dummy. Keep the shape neat, mirroring the shape of the dummy underneath to make a ball.

6 Roll different-sized balls of light green sugarpaste, using 5–20g (just under ¼–¾oz) of paste for each ball. Flatten down the balls then press them over the surface of the cake to make a base for the craters. Use edible glue to secure them in place.

7 Moisten the cake with a little cooled, boiled water or edible glue, ensuring the dummy is well covered so the sugarpaste will stick easily. Roll out the light green sugarpaste and cover the cake completely, smoothing down and around the sphere (see page 20).

8 Push the end of a small rolling pin into each crater then randomly around the cake to make more craters. Push in even deeper where the alien will be popping out of the front of the cake and press a small piece of black modelling paste into the hole to give it depth. To make smaller holes, push the end of a paintbrush randomly into the surface of the cake.

9 Lift the cake carefully and stick it in the centre of the cake board using a little edible glue or a dab of chocolate to secure it in place.

ROCKET

10 To make the stabilizers, roll out the red modelling paste and cut out three 5.5cm (2¼") circles using a cutter. Following the step picture as a guide, use the same cutter to cut a section from each circle. Use a 3.5cm (1⅜") cutter to cut two smaller sections from one side of the larger piece of paste. Roll a tiny, pointed sausage from the trimmings and set aside.

11 Roll out the red sugarpaste and cover the marshmallow rice cereal rocket, smoothing around the shape. Close the join on the underside, cut away any excess if necessary and smooth over the surface with a ball of sugarpaste. Cut out a circle from one side using a 2cm (¾") round cutter and remove the sugarpaste. Roll out some black modelling paste into a thin sheet, cut out a circle of the same size and use it to fill the hole in the rocket.

12 Roll out the orange modelling paste but leave it quite thick, then cut out a 3cm and a 4cm (1⅛" and 1½") circle. Cut a 2cm (¾") circle from the centre of the 3cm (1⅛") circle to make a ring. Secure the larger circle to the back of the rocket, then stick the smaller ring onto it.

13 Split 2g (a pinch) of red modelling paste into four equal pieces and roll them into very small balls. Make an indent in the centre of each one with the end of a paintbrush. Roll each of them again to straighten the sides then stick them inside the ring on the back of the rocket to make the exhaust.

14 To make the flames, divide 5g (just under ¼oz) of yellow modelling paste into four equal pieces. Roll each piece into a tapered sausage and press down to flatten slightly. Make V-shaped cuts into the end of each sausage and stick in position on the rocket exhaust. Dilute some red paste food colour with a little cooled, boiled water until you achieve a watercolour consistency and paint over the middle of the flames.

15 Model a tiny flattened circle from some red modelling paste, make a hole in the centre with a cocktail stick and attach it to the front of the rocket. Insert the tiny, pointed sausage you made earlier into the hole and secure with edible glue.

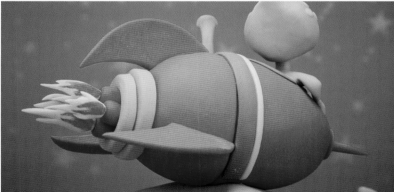

16 Decorate the rocket with strips of yellow and mauve modelling paste. Make a ring from some mauve sugarpaste using 2cm and 3cm (¾" and 1") round cutters and secure over the black circle on top of the rocket. Push the dowel down into the top of the cake and gently push the rocket down onto it, securing at the base with a little edible glue.

SEATED ALIEN

Body

17 To make the seated alien, roll 5g (just under ¼oz) of green modelling paste into an oval shape for the body. Pinch out a neck at the top and push in around the centre of the body to make a waist. Open up the neck area with a cocktail stick, winding it around slightly to open it further. Moisten a lolly stick with edible glue and insert it into the body. Push the lolly stick and the body into the surface of the cake, securing at the bottom with edible glue. Mould the neck area around the lolly stick to ensure it is secure then cut away any excess paste.

Legs

18 Split 5g (just under ¼oz) of green modelling paste in half to make the legs. Roll each piece into a sausage, bend the ends round to make the feet and pinch at the back to bring out the heels. Bend halfway along the paste to make the knees, pushing in deeply and rolling the paste back and forth. Make a cut into each foot for the toes and smooth over them gently to round them off.

Head

19 Roll 15g (½oz) of green modelling paste into a ball, roll out the top of the ball further and pinch out the antenna. Round off the top then push the small end of a ball or bone tool into the top of the antenna.

20 Lay the head flat and smooth over the facial area to flatten it slightly. Push the 2cm (¾") round cutter into the mouth area at an angle to mark on the smile and add a dimple in each corner with the tip of a cocktail stick. Push the small end of a ball or bone tool into the top of the face to make an eye socket. Model a small, flattened oval of white modelling paste, secure it in the socket and position a tiny oval of black modelling paste on top. Roll tiny balls of yellow modelling paste, flatten them down and stick them over the top of the face and the bottom of the antenna.

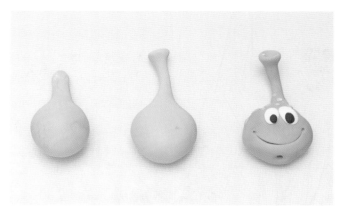

Arms

21 Roll 2g (a pinch) of green modelling paste into a sausage shape and roll gently at the end to round off the hand. Roll out the hand a little further then press down to flatten slightly. Cut the thumb into one side then make two cuts into the top of the hand to separate the fingers. Roll each finger to lengthen it and round off the tips. Push gently halfway up the arm to make the elbow then stick in position on the body. Make another arm in the same way, but cut the thumb into the opposite side.

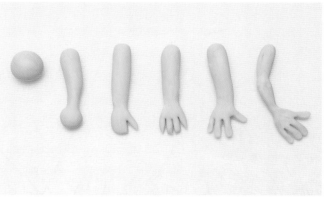

ALIEN IN ROCKET

22 Make the head, neck and arms in the same way as for the seated alien, but give this alien two eyes, as shown in the picture. Insert a lolly stick into the base of the shoulders and stick this into the black part on top of the rocket.

ALIEN IN CRATER

23 Make a head and two hands in the same way as for the seated alien, but give this alien two eyes. Insert a lolly stick into the base of the head and push this into the black crater on the cake. Position the hands in front of the head and secure to the cake.

FINISHING TOUCHES

24 Cut out with the larger cutters or model circles from the remaining modelling paste and stick them over the cake board to look like planets.

25 For the stars, dilute the silver lustre dust with a few drops of lemon extract (or clear alcohol) and dab randomly over the board.

26 Dust each alien with a little bright yellow dust food colour.

27 Trim the edge of the cake board with navy blue ribbon to finish (see page 21).

Alien and Planet Mini Cakes

EDIBLES

Alien (per cake)

7cm (2¾") half-sphere cake (see recipes on pages 6–9)

15g (½oz) cake filling (see recipes on pages 10–12)

Sugarpaste (rolled fondant):

    45g (1½oz) green

    30g (1oz) navy blue

    A little black, white and yellow

Planet (per cake)

2 x 7cm (2½") half-sphere cakes (see recipes on pages 6–9)

30g (1oz) cake filling (see recipes on pages 10–12)

Sugarpaste (rolled fondant):

    75g (2½oz) in the colour of your choice for covering

    30g (1oz) navy blue

    20g (¾oz) green

    A little black, yellow, white and other colours of your choice

EQUIPMENT

Basic equipment (see pages 15–17)

10cm (4") round cake card

Lolly stick (for planet cake)

TIP

If you prefer, you could use marshmallow rice cereal instead of cake to make these alien-themed party bag treats.

ALIEN

1 Cover the cake card with navy blue sugarpaste and set aside.

2 Cover the half-sphere cake with green sugarpaste, smoothing around the shape. Push up the excess sugarpaste towards the top of the head to make the antenna and bend it upwards. Smooth around the edge of the cake then stick it onto the cake card.

3 Add the facial features in the same way as for the aliens on the main cake, using a larger cutter to make the smile. Decorate with different-sized yellow spots.

PLANET

1 Cover the cake card with navy blue sugarpaste and set aside.

2 Sandwich two half-sphere cakes together with a little cake filling, then spread more cake filling over the surface of the cake. Stick small circles of sugarpaste over the cake for the craters, then cover in the same way as for the cake in the main project. Push the end of a small rolling pin into the top of the cake to make a deep crater.

3 Model an alien head and hands from green sugarpaste following the instructions in the main project. Secure the head into the crater on the top of the cake and position the hands in front of the head.

4 Decorate the cake card with small circles of sugarpaste in different colours.

Princess Carriage

This pretty-in-pink princess carriage will certainly make a special surprise for the belle of the ball. The top half of the carriage is made from cake and the bottom half from polystyrene, which is ideal if you don't need as many servings but still want the cake to look impressive. If you've got lots of mouths to feed, simply replace the polystyrene dummy with another dome-shaped cake.

EDIBLES

20cm (8") half-sphere or bowl-shaped cake, 4.5cm (1¾") deep (see recipes on pages 6–9)

20cm (8") round cake, 4.5cm (1¾") deep (see recipes on pages 6–9)

350g (12¼oz) cake filling (see recipes on pages 10–12)

200g (7oz) chocolate ganache or melted white chocolate (see page 12)

100g (3½oz) marshmallow rice cereal (see page 11)

Edible glue (see page 14)

Liquid food colour: black (SK)

Dust (powder) food colour: pale pink (SK)

Lustre dust (powder) food colours: gold and silver (SK)

1–2tsp lemon extract (or clear alcohol, e.g. gin or vodka)

Sugarpaste (rolled fondant):

    1kg (2lb 3¼oz) pink

    315g (11oz) pale pink

    20g (¾oz) grey

Modelling paste (see page 14):

    175g (6oz) pink

    160g (5½oz) pale pink

    45g (1½oz) grey

    35g (1¼oz) cream

    30g (1oz) skin tone

    5g (¼oz) blue

    5g (¼oz) green

    5g (¼oz) white

    Pinch of black

EQUIPMENT

Basic equipment (see pages 15–17)

30cm (12") round cake board

1m x 15mm width (40" x ⅝") satin ribbon: pink

20cm (8") round cake card

20cm (8") half-sphere polystyrene dummy

Round cutter: 9cm (3½")

24-gauge floral wires: white

8 paper lolly sticks

Template (see page 147)

CAKE BOARD

1 Cover the cake board with pale pink sugarpaste (see page 21).

MARSHMALLOW RICE CEREAL HEAD AND DRESS

2 Roll 30g (1oz) of the marshmallow rice cereal into a 4cm (1½") ball for the princess' head. Shape the remaining marshmallow rice cereal into a 9cm (3½") tall cone for the skirt. Press it down on a work surface to flatten the base and set aside for later.

CAKE

3 Level the top of the cakes and cut each of them into two layers. Assemble the layers with the domed cake on top and trim down the sides with a serrated knife to make a neat dome shape. Trim no more than 1cm (⅜") into the front of the cake where the carriage door will be, slicing down to the bottom. Sandwich the layers together with the cake filling of your choice and attach a cake card to the base of the cake.

4 Use a serrated knife to cut a small amount off the top of the half-sphere dummy to create a flat base. Do this in a separate room away from the cake and wipe away any polystyrene particles.

5 Place the cake onto the flat, wider side of the half-sphere dummy. Spread a layer of ganache or melted chocolate over the surface of the cake and the join between the cake and the dummy. Keep the shape

neat, mirroring the shape of the dummy underneath to make a ball. Set aside to firm.

WHEELS

Important note: I have used floral wires to support the wheels as they are fragile and could break. If you are confident that your modelling paste will dry firm enough then you can omit the supports. Where you have used floral wires or other inedible supports, always ensure that you inform the recipient so that they are removed safely before the cake is served.

6 Twist four floral wires into spirals for the wheels, making two of them slightly more open so they are larger. The two smaller wheels for the front of the carriage should be 8cm (3⅛") in diameter and the two slightly larger wheels for the back should be 9cm (3½") in diameter.

7 Roll 10g (¼oz) of pale pink modelling paste into a long, thin sausage that is 40cm (16") long and tapers at either end. Press down on the paste with a cake smoother to flatten it. Moisten one of the wire wheels with edible glue and carefully cover it with the sausage of paste, curling it around the centre. Press down on it to embed the wire into the back of the paste. Cover the remaining three wheels in the same way and set aside until dry.

8 Paint the front of all four carriage wheels with gold lustre dust mixed with lemon extract (or clear alcohol) and set aside to dry. Once dry, flip them over and paint the reverse.

CARRIAGE

9 Moisten the cake and dummy with a little cooled, boiled water or edible glue, ensuring the dummy is well covered so the sugarpaste will stick easily. Roll out the pink sugarpaste and cover the cake completely, smoothing down and around the shape (see page 20). Cut away the carriage window from the front of the cake using the template as a guide. Roll out some pale grey sugarpaste into a thin sheet, cut out a window using the same template and fill in the space at the front of the cake.

10 To mark on the carriage door, press the 9cm (3½") round cutter into the paste just below the window then make an indent down the centre with a knife. Use the edge of a ruler to indent a line vertically down the middle of the carriage, then mark two more evenly spaced lines in each half to make six sections. You need to indent six lines around the carriage to ensure it is symmetrical.

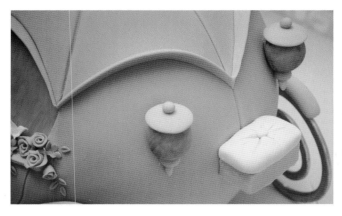

11 Split 30g (1oz) of pink modelling paste into six even pieces. Roll each piece into a long, tapering sausage and press down with a cake smoother to flatten. Smooth over the front edge to thin it out further and cut the back edge straight if required. Position the first piece around the top edge of the window and secure with edible glue. Attach the remaining pieces around the carriage in the same way, mirroring the shape of the first.

12 Cut a small strip of pink modelling paste for the window ledge and attach it to the top of the door. Roll two tiny pink sausages, curl them up and attach them to the door as handles.

LAMPS

13 Insert two lolly sticks into either side of the cake where the lamps will be positioned, leaving approximately 1cm (³/₈") of each stick protruding. Split the grey modelling paste into four equal pieces, roll into ball shapes and push gently onto each lolly stick. Place a flattened disc of pink paste on top of each lamp, top with a tiny ball of paste then attach a cone shape under each one.

14 Dilute the black liquid food colour with a little cooled, boiled water to make a translucent grey shade. Paint a wash of colour over the window and lamps.

SEAT

15 Push two lolly sticks into one side of the carriage for the seat, spacing them 3cm (1¹/₈") apart on either side of the indented line. Leave approximately 1.5cm (⁵/₈") of each lolly stick protruding from the cake. Roll out 30g (1oz) of pink modelling paste to 1.5cm (⁵/₈") thick and cut out a rectangle that is 2.5cm x 4cm (1" x 1½") in size. Moisten the lolly sticks with edible glue, then push the rectangle onto the sticks until it touches the side of the carriage. Attach a

small, flattened disc to the underside with a tiny teardrop of pink modelling paste.

16 Roll 20g (¾oz) of pale pink modelling paste into an oval shape for the seat cushion and press down gently to flatten it slightly. Mark the pleats across the top with a small knife and attach a tiny ball of paste in the centre. Stick in position so it is resting on top of the seat and secured against the sides of the carriage.

CROWN

17 For the crown on top of the carriage, roll a 5g (just under ¼oz) ball of pink modelling paste and flatten it down. Roll out 20g (¾oz) of pink paste into a thin sheet and cut it to 4cm x 8cm (1½" x 3¹/₈") in size. Cut V-shapes along the top of the paste to make five points for the crown. Moisten the flattened circle with edible glue then curl the second piece of paste around it with the points facing upwards. Secure at the join, leave to firm for a few moments then stroke the tips so they curve outwards.

18 Mix a little gold lustre dust with a few drops of lemon extract (or clear alcohol) and paint over the gold crown with a no. 4 paintbrush. Roll a 5g (just under ¼oz) ball of pink modelling paste, place it in the centre of the crown and secure two tiny balls of paste on top.

FLOWERS

TIP

These handmade flowers are very quick to make, but you could always use a miniature flower cutter to make them even quicker.

19 To make a rose, roll a small pea-sized piece of pink modelling paste into a long sausage. Press your index finger across the top

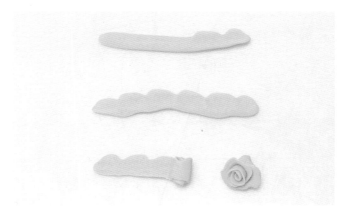

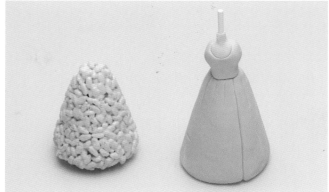

of the paste, pulling the paste out slightly to make at least six petal shapes. Roll the paste up tightly from one end then turn out the petals at the top. Roll tiny teardrops of green modelling paste and indent the centre of each one with a cocktail stick to make the rose leaves.

20 For the white flowers, roll tiny teardrop shapes of white modelling paste and press them onto the handle of a paintbrush. Make four even cuts around the flower, cutting against the paintbrush handle. Remove and pinch the petals gently, then push the paintbrush handle into the centre to shape the flower. Make the blue flowers in the same way but round off the tip of each petal.

21 Attach the flowers and leaves across the top of the window ledge using a little edible glue.

CHASSIS

22 Carefully stick the wheels in position on the carriage, holding for a few moments to secure. Split 35g (1¼oz) of pink modelling paste in half and roll into 24cm (9½") long sausages that are slightly thicker at the ends. Stick one in place against the front of the carriage so it sits below the door, then bring the ends up to rest on top of each wheel. Attach the second piece across the back in the same way.

PRINCESS

Dress

23 Roll out 75g (2½oz) of pink modelling paste into a 15cm (6") diameter circle. Wrap the paste around the marshmallow rice cereal cone you made earlier, stretching out any pleats and smoothing downwards. Smooth the surface with a ball of trimmings then use a ruler to indent deep pleats down either side of the front of her skirt. Mark pleat lines around the top of the skirt in the same way using a cocktail stick.

TIP

If there are stubborn pleats as you are covering the cone, cut them away and smooth the join closed or incorporate them into the pleats of the dress.

24 Roll 10g (¼oz) of pink modelling paste into a ball for the bodice. Place the ball on a work surface then roll it back and forth from the centre using your finger, narrowing one end and rounding off the top. Push a ball or bone tool into the neck/chest area and cut the bottom straight. Stick the bodice onto the top of the skirt. Make a hole down through the bodice using a cocktail stick and open it up ready for the support. Moisten the lolly stick with edible glue then push gently but firmly down through the bodice and cone, leaving a little protruding to support the neck and head.

25 For the sleeves, split 5g (just under ¼oz) of pink modelling paste in half then roll two small, tapered sausages that are each 4.5cm (1¾") long. Hollow out the narrower end of each sleeve with the handle of a paintbrush then stick the sleeves in position so that her arms are crossed with one shoulder slightly forward.

Neck and chest

26 Roll 2g (a pinch) of skin-tone modelling paste into a ball and pinch half of the ball into a neck shape. Flatten down the lower half and attach to the front of the bodice to make the chest. Make a hole in the top of the neck using a cocktail stick and twist to open it up further. Moisten a lolly stick with edible glue then gently insert it down through the neck, bodice and into the skirt, leaving a little protruding to support the head. Smooth the neck against the lolly stick and cut away any excess if necessary.

Hands

27 Roll a pea-sized piece of skin tone modelling paste into a teardrop shape and flatten it slightly, smoothing gently around the outside edge. Make a straight cut into one side of the rounded end of the paste for the thumb, making sure to cut no further than halfway down. Make three slightly shorter cuts along the top to separate the fingers. Roll each finger gently to lengthen and round them off, then squeeze them together. Push the thumb down towards the palm to shape the hand. Roll gently at the wrist to lengthen it slightly then stick the hand into the sleeve with a little edible glue. Hold in place for a few moments until secure. Repeat to make a second hand in the same way, cutting the thumb into the opposite side.

Head

28 Roll the marshmallow rice cereal ball for the head back and forth over the work surface to flatten the face area slightly. Roll out 15g (½oz) of skin-tone modelling paste and use it to cover the marshmallow rice cereal ball completely (no need to neaten this as it will all be covered with hair later). Gently push the head down onto the lolly stick protruding from the neck and secure with edible glue.

29 To make the face, first set aside a tiny ball of skin-tone modelling paste for the nose, then roll the remaining skin tone paste into a ball. Press down on the paste to flatten it, smoothing around the outside edge. Pinch at the bottom to create a chin. Add a tiny strip of pink modelling paste for her mouth and mark a line across the centre to separate the top and bottom lips. Use a cocktail stick to add dimples in the corners of the mouth and push down gently to shape the Cupid's bow on her top lip.

30 Attach the tiny ball for the nose just above the mouth, then indent the nostrils with a cocktail stick.

31 Indent two eye sockets using a ball or bone tool. Roll two small balls of white modelling paste and two tiny balls of blue and black paste. Flatten down the balls and stick two white discs in the eye sockets, then attach the blue and black discs to make the iris and pupil on each eye. Roll two very thin, black tapered sausages for the eyelashes and secure on top of the eyes. Make the eyebrows in the same way using cream modelling paste and attach to the face.

32 Stick the face onto the front of the head, ensuring there is room at the top for the hair, then smooth in place following the contours of the face.

33 For the hair, build up long, tapering sausages of cream modelling paste around the princess' head, starting at the crown and following the outline of the face. Give the hair texture with the handle of a paintbrush as you attach each strand. Ensure each strand is stuck against her back otherwise they may stretch and break off. Add smaller pieces at the front to frame her face and create a central parting.

34 Model several tiny ovals and balls and use them to build up the tiara then paint them with the gold lustre dust mixture.

FINISHING TOUCHES

35 Use the gold dust mixture to add a tiny highlight to each eye at the one o'clock position and paint the carriage door handles. Stipple some gold paint around the bottom of her dress. Brush a light covering of silver lustre dust over the princess and the carriage to add some sparkle. Dust a little pale pink dust food colour over her cheeks to add some blush.

36 Trim the edge of the board with pink ribbon to finish (see page 21).

Mini Carriage Cakes

EDIBLES
(per cake)

2 x 7cm (2¾") half-sphere cakes (see recipes on pages 6–9)

20g (¾oz) cake filling (see recipes on pages 10–12)

20g (¾oz) ganache or melted white chocolate (see page 12)

Lustre dust (powder) food colour: silver (SK)

Sugarpaste (rolled fondant) in colours of your choice:

    45g (1½oz) for the cake

    25g (just over ¾oz) for the cake card

Modelling paste (see page 14):

    10g (¼oz) colour of your choice for details on carriage

    5g (just under ¼oz) grey

    2g (pinch) skin tone

    2g (pinch) hair colour

    Tiny pinch of black

EQUIPMENT
(per cake)

Basic equipment (see pages 15–17)

10cm (4") round cake card

Piping nozzle (tip): no. 4 (PME) or small drinking straw

1 Cover the cake card with approximately 25g (just over ¾oz) of sugarpaste in the colour of your choice and set aside.

2 Stick the two half-sphere cakes together with a little cake filling then spread ganache or melted chocolate over the outside of the cake. Roll out approximately 45g (1½oz) of sugarpaste in the colour of your choice and cover the cake, smoothing down and around the sphere (see page 20).

3 Mark six equal sections around the cake with a ruler, then cut away the window and replace with grey sugarpaste in the same way as for the main cake.

4 To decorate the carriage, model smaller, simplified versions of the lamps, window ledge, window arch, seat, chassis and wheels from modelling paste in colours of your choice, using the main cake as a guide. Attach them to the cake with edible glue.

5 Roll a small ball of skin-tone-coloured modelling paste and flatten it slightly to make a face. Model some hair around the face. Roll two tiny ovals of black modelling paste for the eyes and a tiny ball of skin-tone-coloured paste for the nose. Mark on the mouth using a no. 4 piping nozzle or a small straw, then secure the face to the carriage window with a little edible glue.

6 Lightly brush the carriage with silver lustre dust to finish.

Farmyard Fun

This simple barn with cute farm animals peeking out makes a really lovely centrepiece, without being too time-consuming. If you have more time, the addition of the farmer on his tractor and the pig in his pen complete the scene perfectly.

EDIBLES

30cm (12") square cake, 6cm (2") deep (see recipes on pages 6–9)

350g (12¼oz) cake filling (see recipes on pages 10–12)

250g (8¾oz) chocolate ganache or melted white chocolate (see page 12)

Edible glue (see page 14)

Sugarpaste (rolled fondant):

    550g (1lb 3½oz) red

    315g (11oz) pale green

    300g (10½oz) pale grey

    75g (2½oz) black

    50g (1¾oz) beige

Modelling paste (see page 14):

    110g (3¾oz) white

    100g (3½oz) golden brown

    60g (2oz) dark green

    50g (1¾oz) black

    40g (1½oz) pale pink

    35g (1¼oz) pale yellow

    30g (1oz) yellow

    25g (just over ¾oz) cream

    10g (¼oz) pale red

EQUIPMENT

Basic equipment (see pages 15–17)

30cm (12") round cake board

1 x 10cm (4") and 2 x 2.5cm (1") long sugar sticks plus a few extra, or lengths of raw, dried spaghetti (see page 14)

Square cutter: 4cm (1½")

Small round cutter

Templates (see page 148)

1m x 15mm width (40" x ⅝") satin ribbon: green

CAKE BOARD

1 Cover the cake board with pale green sugarpaste (see page 21). Smooth over the surface with a cake smoother then press a large rolling pin over the board to create ripples. Trim any excess paste from around the edge and set aside to dry.

WEATHERVANE

2 Roll out the black modelling paste into a thin sheet then use the templates and the tip of a knife to cut out the shape of the weathervane. To support the weathervane, moisten a sugar stick or length of raw, dried spaghetti with a little edible glue and cover it with the rolled-out black modelling paste. Roll over the surface to close the join and cut away 5cm (2") of paste from the bottom. Stick this support to the back of the weathervane with the uncovered part at the bottom and set aside to dry.

CAKE

3 Remove the crust and level the top of the cake. Measure the cake carefully then cut it into four equal squares, cutting it in half and then half again. Stack the squares on top of each other.

4 To shape the roof, measure 2cm (¾") down each side of the top cake. Starting in the centre of the top cake, curve the knife down and out to this point, creating a rounded groove. Repeat again to make another groove below the first, then cut down slightly further so you remove the top edge of the second layer. Repeat on the opposite side. Trim down the sides of the cake to make them curve inwards slightly.

5 Cut each square cake into two layers then sandwich the cakes back together with cake filling; the total height of the cake should be approximately 20cm (8"). Spread the surface of the cake with softened chocolate ganache, taking care to keep the covering as smooth as possible. To achieve a sharp edge, first coat the opposite sides of the cake up to the roof, then cover the back and front to give the sides time to set.

6 Roll out the red sugarpaste and cut out two pieces big enough to cover the sides of the cake, but only to the bottom of the roof. Cover the front and back in the same way, this time to the top of the roof, then trim the top of the paste to the shape of the roof. Run the tip of a knife vertically over the surface of the sugarpaste to create a woodgrain effect and help disguise the joins.

7 Roll out the grey sugarpaste to a thickness of 3–4mm ($1/8$") and cut out a rectangle that is slightly larger than the surface of the roof so there is a slight overhang. Carefully pick up the sugarpaste, taking care not to distort the shape, then place it over the top of the cake and smooth around the shape to define the ridges.

TIP

If the sugarpaste stretches along the edge, simply hold a cake smoother under the edge and cut down through the paste carefully, taking care not to damage the smoother.

8 Use the templates to cut out the door and the window at the front of the barn and use the square cutter to cut out the windows on the sides. Roll out some more black sugarpaste into a thin sheet, use the templates again to cut out the door and window shapes and fill the uncovered areas. Trim the top of the barn door and the windows with a thin strip of grey sugarpaste.

9 Roll out the golden-brown modelling paste and cut out a rectangle that is 6cm ($2^3/8$") long and the same width as the barn door opening, using the template as a guide. Press the edge of a ruler evenly over the surface to mark on the wooden planks and stick in place with a little cooled, boiled water or edible glue. Add a strip of golden-brown sugarpaste across the top of the door and two more crossed diagonally over the front and mark on the woodgrain effect as before. Use the trimmings to make the window ledges and secure in place.

PATH

10 Roll out the beige sugarpaste and use the template to cut out the shape of the pathway, smoothing around the edge to soften and flatten out the paste. Stick in place at the front of the doorway, trimming any excess from around the cake board edge. Press a small rolling pin across the surface a few times to give it texture.

HEN

11 To make the hen's nest, roll 20g (¾oz) of pale yellow modelling paste into an oval and snip into the surface with small scissors to create a straw-like texture. Stick in place on the ledge of the top window.

12 For the hen, roll 10g (¼oz) of white modelling paste into an oval and make two indents on either side with the end of a paintbrush to mark the feathers. Stick in place on top of the nest, resting against the window opening.

13 Roll the pale red modelling paste into a ball for the head and pinch out the neck area, bringing it down into a point at the front, then stick in position. Roll a tiny pale red sausage for the comb and make two indents in it with the end of a paintbrush. Use yellow modelling paste to make a pointed teardrop shape for the beak and snip just underneath the point to separate the top and bottom. Mark the nostrils using a cocktail stick and add two tiny ovals of black modelling paste for the eyes.

COW

14 Make a flattened teardrop from 10g (¼oz) of white modelling paste for the shoulders, stick it against the barn door opening and add a small, flattened black patch. Roll 35g (1¼oz) of white modelling paste into a rounded teardrop for the head, using the fuller part as the top. Push a bone tool into the narrower end to open the mouth and pull it down gently. For the patch, roll out a pinch of black modelling paste and attach it to the head so it covers one eye. Shape two black teardrops for the ears, make an indent in each one with a bone tool then add a small, flattened teardrop of pink modelling paste in the centre. Attach to either side of the cow's head.

15 For the muzzle, roll 5g (just under ¼oz) of white modelling paste into a small sausage, make a slight indent in the centre to narrow it then push a bone tool into each rounded end. Add two pink teardrop shapes on either side and push into the paste with a bone tool again. Stick the muzzle in position so it just covers the top of the mouth area and secure with edible glue. Add two tiny black ovals for the eyes.

SHEEP

16 Roll 5g (just under ¼oz) of cream modelling paste into a ball for the shoulders and flatten it slightly. Stick it against the barn door opening to the left of the cow. Roll 20g (¾oz) of cream modelling

paste into a teardrop shape for the sheep's head then indent the mouth with a small, round cutter. Make a line from the mouth to the nose area with the back of a knife. Push the end of a paintbrush into the bottom of the mouth and pull down gently. Indent two eye sockets with the end of a paintbrush and add two tiny ovals of black modelling paste for the eyes.

17 Roll several small balls of white modelling paste for the woolly coat and flatten them down. Stick them over the top of the head and cover the shoulders. Roll an oval of pale pink modelling paste for the nose and make two ears in the same way as for the cow, but omit the pink centres.

PIG

18 Roll 5g (just under ¼oz) of pale pink modelling paste into a ball and flatten slightly for the pig's body. Stick in position against the barn door. Roll 20g (¾oz) of pink modelling paste into a rounded teardrop for the head, open the mouth in the same way as for the cow then stick in position with a little edible glue. Model a small triangular snout, round off the edges and indent the nostrils with the end of a paintbrush. Indent two eye sockets using the end of a paintbrush and add two tiny ovals of black modelling paste for the eyes. Use the leftover pale pink modelling paste to make the ears in the same way as for the sheep.

DOG

19 Roll 20g (¾oz) of white modelling paste into a fat sausage and pinch out the legs, gently rolling out each one to the same length. Bend the end of each leg forward slightly to make the paws. Carefully pinch out the neck then insert a sugar stick into it and secure with a little edible glue. Set aside to dry.

TIP

If the paste seems too soft to support the body, try adding another pinch or two of CMC to the modelling paste. Alternatively, insert a sugar stick into each leg and roll the paste down over the stick, securing with a tiny dab of edible glue.

20 For the dog's head, roll 10g (¼oz) of white modelling paste into a rounded teardrop, then make the mouth and nose in the same way as for the sheep.

21 When the body is dry, roll out some black modelling paste into a thin sheet, cut out several patches and stick them over the body. Indent the eye area with the end of a paintbrush and add two tiny

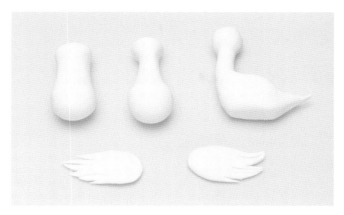

ovals of black modelling paste for the eyes. Model a long, tapering sausage of black paste for the tail, push a sugar stick into the end and insert it into the dog's back. Make two ears from black modelling paste in the same way as for the sheep.

MOTHER DUCK AND DUCKLINGS

22   Use 10g (¼oz) of white modelling paste for the mother duck's body and split the remaining yellow modelling paste into five equal pieces for each duckling. Roll the white modelling paste into a ball for the mother duck then gently pinch up the neck and round off the head. Stroke the opposite end of the body to create the tail feathers, curving them upwards. Lay the shape flat until the neck has firmed up, then stand it up and leave to dry completely. Make the ducklings' bodies in the same way.

23   Model flattened teardrop shapes for the wings, cut into the pointed end with a knife and secure to the sides of the duck. Roll a small teardrop of orange modelling paste for the beak and stick the rounded end to the bottom of the face. Use small scissors to snip just below the point of the beak to open it up. Indent eye sockets with the end of a paintbrush and add tiny ovals of black modelling paste as before. Add a small teardrop or two of white modelling paste to the top of the duck's head to make a tuft of feathers. Alternatively, you can snip into the top of the head with small scissors to make the tuft. Roll two tiny teardrops from orange modelling paste, cut twice into the rounded end to make webbed feet and secure to the bottom of the duck's body.

24   Make the ducklings in the same way using yellow modelling paste, but omit the feet.

FINISHING TOUCHES

25   Push the weathervane down into the roof and secure with a dab of edible glue.

26   Roll out the dark green modelling paste, leaving it quite thick. Push the back of a knife into the top of the paste twice to make the shape of a bush, moving the knife back and forth to open up a V-shape. Cut the bottom and one side of the paste straight then stick the bush in place against the side of the barn.

27   Trim the edge of the cake board with green ribbon to finish (see page 21).

Pig Pen Mini Cake

EDIBLES
(per cake)

6cm x 5cm (2³⁄₈" x 2")
rectangular cake, 4cm (1½")
deep (see recipes on pages 6–9)

75g (2½oz) cake filling (see
recipes on pages 10–12)

Sugarpaste (rolled fondant):

    75g (2½oz) light brown

    50g (1¾oz) dark brown

Modelling paste (see page 14):

    20g (¾oz) pale pink

    5g (¼oz) black

EQUIPMENT
(per cake)

Basic equipment (see pages
15–17)

15cm (6") round cake card
(or similar)

Sugar stick or short length of
raw, dried spaghetti

Template (see page 148)

1 Cut the cake card to shape using the template as a guide, cover it with dark brown sugarpaste and set aside to dry.

2 Trim the top of the cake at an angle so it top slopes down by no more than 1cm (³⁄₈"). Layer and fill the cake then spread cake filling over the surface.

3 Roll out the light brown sugarpaste and cut out lengths to cover the two opposite sides first, then the front and back of the pen. Add lines with a ruler and create a woodgrain effect with a small knife. Cut out the doorway and fill with rolled-out black modelling paste. Cover the roof in the same way as the sides, making the lengths slightly larger than the top of the cake. Add a small strip over the top of the doorway.

4 Use half of the pink modelling paste to make the pig's body in the same way as the dog on the main cake. Press a knife into the end of each leg to mark the trotters. Gently pinch out the neck area and insert a small sugar stick to help support the head. Lay the body flat until the paste has firmed.

5 Make the head, muzzle, ears and eyes in the same way as for the pig on the main cake. Curl up a tiny sausage of pink modelling paste for the tail and attach it to the body. Use the leftover dark brown paste to make cloud-shaped mud splashes and stick them over the pig and pig pen.

Tractor Mini Cake

EDIBLES
(per cake)

11cm x 4cm (4¼" x 1½")
rectangular cake, trimmed
and levelled (see recipes on
pages 6–9)

150g (5¼oz) cake filling (see
recipes on pages 10–12)

Dust (powder) food colour:
red (SK)

Sugarpaste (rolled fondant):

    135g (4¾oz) red

    90g (3oz) green

Modelling paste (see page 14):

    115g (4oz) black

    15g (½oz) white

15g (½oz) skin tone

10g (¼oz) blue

Small piece of grey and brown

EQUIPMENT
(per cake)

Basic equipment (see
pages 15–17)

12cm x 5cm (5" x 2") rectangular
cake card

15cm (6") round cake card

Round cutters: 1.5cm, 3cm and
4cm (⁵⁄₈", 1¹⁄₈" and 1½")

Paper lolly stick: 10cm (4") long

Piping nozzle (tip): no. 18 (PME)
(or miniature round cutter)

TRACTOR

1 To elevate the tractor, split 20g (¾oz) of green sugarpaste in half and roll each piece into a long sausage. Stick them in parallel across the centre of the cake card, 5cm (2") apart. Roll out the remaining green sugarpaste and cover the cake card completely, smoothing the paste around the strips. Trim any excess from around the edge.

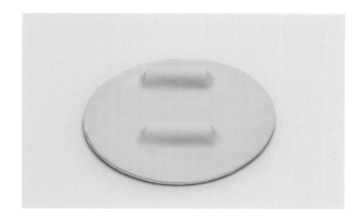

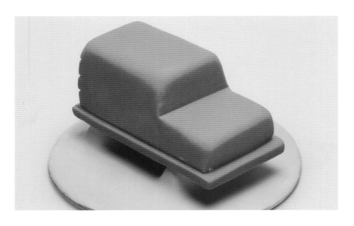
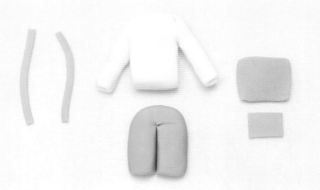

2 Roll out 60g (2oz) of red sugarpaste to 5mm (¼") thick and stick the small rectangular cake card down onto it with edible glue. Cut around the paste so it is slightly larger than the card, turn over and set aside to dry.

3 Cut a 4cm long x 2cm deep (1½" x ¾") piece from one end of the cake to make the tractor seat. Spread a layer of cake filling over the surface. Roll out the remaining red sugarpaste and cover the cake completely, smoothing down and around the shape. Use a ruler to indent grille lines across the larger end then position the cake on the covered cake card.

4 To make the back wheels, split 75g (2½oz) of black modelling paste in half and roll each piece into a ball. Press down with a cake smoother until they are both approximately 6cm (2³⁄₈") in diameter. Split 15g (½oz) in half for the smaller wheels and press down until they are 3cm (1¹⁄₈") in diameter. Push a smaller round cutter into the centre of each wheel, smoothing the paste with your fingers. Cut out circles from rolled-out red modelling paste and stick in the centre of each wheel. Stick the wheels in position once they have firmed.

5 Set aside a tiny piece of black modelling paste, then use the remainder to model a rectangle for the seat, a strip for the front bumper, a cylinder for the funnel and a small steering wheel. Model two round headlights from white modelling paste and two wheel arches from red modelling paste. Add a tiny sausage of grey modelling paste to the top of the funnel and indent the centre with a cocktail stick.

FARMER

6 Use the blue modelling paste to make the farmer's dungarees, following the step photograph as a guide. Model the legs first then make the shirt from white modelling paste, making sure it's the same width as the top of the legs. Use the remaining blue paste to make the bib, pocket and straps. Assemble the farmer's body so he is sitting on the tractor seat then insert a paper lolly stick down into the torso, leaving 1–2cm (³⁄₈–¾") protruding from the neck. Roll two pea-sized pieces of skin-tone modelling paste into teardrops for the hands, flatten them slightly and separate the fingers. Stick against the end of each sleeve.

7 Set aside a pea-sized piece of skin-tone modelling paste then roll the remainder into a ball for the head. Push the top half gently upwards to narrow and round off the cheeks then pinch at the bottom to create a chin. Mark the mouth with a piping nozzle and indent the eye sockets with the end of a paintbrush. Add two tiny ovals of black modelling paste for the eyes and a small oval of skin-tone modelling paste for the nose. Roll two balls of skin-tone paste for the ears and make an indent in the centre with the end of a paintbrush. Brush the cheeks and nose with a little red dust food colour. Add a tiny white highlight to each eye at the one o'clock position.

8 Cut out a circle of yellow modelling paste using a 4cm (1½") round cutter then make cuts in the surface with a knife and tear the edge of the paste. Shape the top of the hat from the remaining yellow paste and make cuts in the surface as before. Stick in position then add tiny pieces of brown modelling paste around the join to make his hair.

Duckling Cupcakes

EDIBLES
(per cupcake)

Cupcake baked in green cupcake case (see recipes on pages 6–9)

20g (¾oz) cake filling (see recipes on pages 10–12)

Sugarpaste (rolled fondant):

    30g (1oz) yellow

Modelling paste (see page 14):

    20g (¾oz) dark yellow

    A little orange and black

EQUIPMENT
(per cupcake)

Basic equipment (see pages 15–17)

Round cutter (to fit cupcake once shaped with cake filling)

1 Bake as many cupcakes as required then spread cake filling over the top in a dome shape.

2 Cut out a circle of yellow sugarpaste and place it on top of the cupcake. Snip into the sugarpaste with small scissors to create a straw-like effect.

3 Make a duckling following the instructions for the main cake and attach it to the top of the cupcake with edible glue.

Friendly Robot

Little ones will love this fun, friendly robot and he is easier to make than you might think. I've used acrylic cake separators for the legs which create a stable base for the cake to sit on and marshmallow rice cereal for the head, making it light enough to rest on top. Have fun customising your own robot with easy-to-make buttons, cogs and dials!

EDIBLES

3 x 15cm (6") square cakes, 5cm (2") deep (see recipes on pages 6–9)

350g (12¼oz) cake filling (see recipes on pages 10–12)

200g (7oz) chocolate ganache or melted white chocolate (see page 12)

340g (12oz) marshmallow rice cereal (see page 11)

Edible glue (see page 14)

30g (1oz) royal icing (see page 13)

Lustre dust (powder) food colours: gold and silver (SK)

1tbsp of lemon extract (or clear alcohol, e.g. gin or vodka)

Sugarpaste (rolled fondant):

    750g (1lb 10½oz) blue

    315g (11oz) cream

Modelling paste:

    600g (1lb 5¼oz) lilac

    360g (12½oz) grey

    210g (7½oz) blue

    30g (1oz) red

    30g (1oz) cream

    2g (pinch) black

EQUIPMENT

Basic equipment (see pages 15–17)

2 x acrylic cake separators: 10cm high x 7cm wide (at top and base) x 3cm (4" x 2¾" x 1¼") diameter tube (or similar)

30cm (12") round cake board

1m x 15mm (40" x ⅝") width ribbon: striped

15cm x 12cm (6" x 5") rectangular cake card (can be cut from a 15cm (6") square cake card)

Food-safe cake dowel: 20cm (8") long

Paper lolly sticks: 1 x 8cm (3⅛"), 2 x 6cm (2⅜") long

Round cutters: 2cm, 2.5cm and 3.5cm (¾", 1", 1⅜")

Piping nozzles (tips): nos. 1.5 and 17 (PME)

Small piece of card (optional)

CAKE BOARD

1 Cover the cake board with 315g (11oz) of cream sugarpaste (see page 21). Sprinkle the surface of the board with gold lustre dust, rub gently in a circular motion with your fingers and set aside to dry.

CAKE

2 Trim the crust from each cake, level the tops and stack together. To make the robot's body, cut 2.5cm (1") from one side to make a rectangular cake (this shorter measurement will be the depth of the body) then place the bottom layer on the cake card and secure with a little cake filling. Sandwich the remaining layers together with cake filling, taking care to keep each layer level.

3 Spread a layer of softened ganache or melted white chocolate over the surface of the cake to seal in any crumbs. To help keep the corners neat, cover opposite sides first, then remove any excess ganache/chocolate carefully before covering the other two opposite sides. Cover the top of the cake last.

LEGS

4 To cover the central part of each acrylic separator, moisten them with a little edible glue then press 60g (2oz) of grey modelling paste against each one. Mould the paste around the separators until they're both completely covered, leaving a 2cm (¾") gap at the top. Smooth the join closed, adding a little edible glue if necessary, then rub over the surface with a small ball of sugarpaste. Use the edge of a ruler to mark evenly spaced rings around the legs, running your fingertips over the rings to open them further.

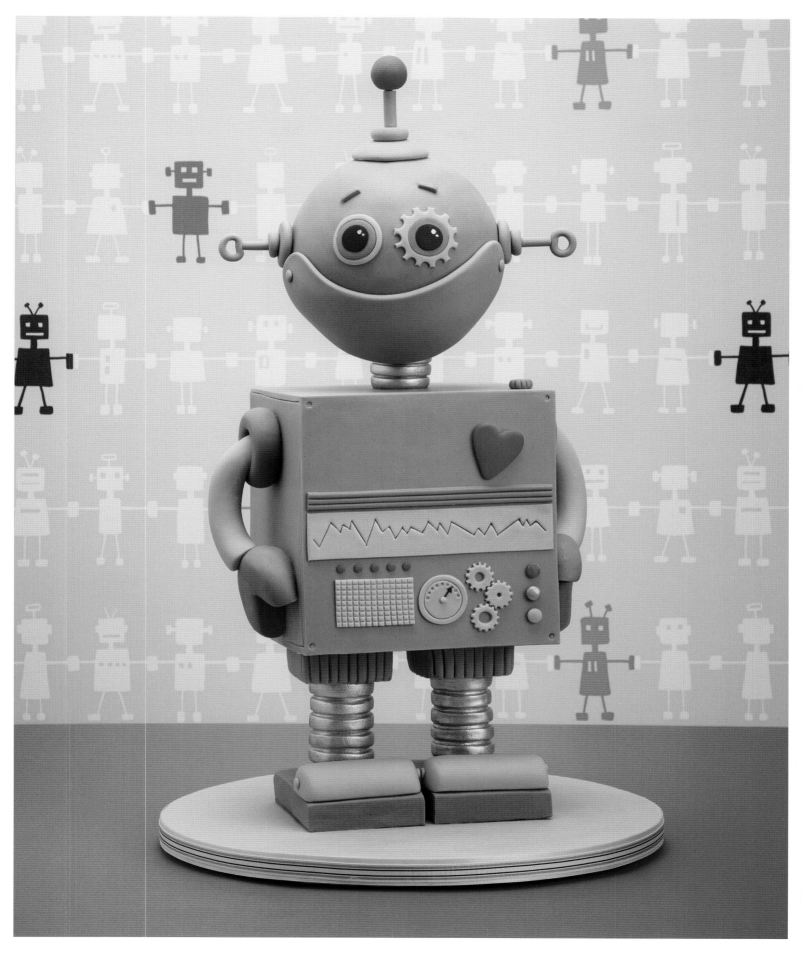

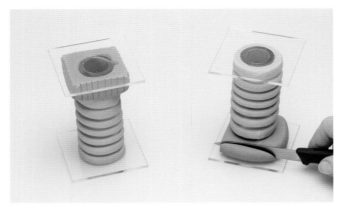

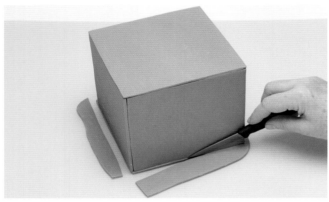

5 Roll out 160g (5½oz) of blue modelling paste to a 2cm (¾") thickness and cut out two squares that are approximately 5cm (2") in size. Use a round cutter to cut a 2.5cm (1") circle from the centre of each square, which should be the same size as the separator column. Moisten under the top of each separator with a little edible glue, cut the squares open so they can be wrapped around the separator and stick in place. Trim the edges of the squares straight with a small, sharp knife. Push the back of a knife into the paste to indent lines around the outside of each piece. Leave to dry upside down.

TORSO

6 To cover the cake, roll out 100g (3½oz) of blue sugarpaste and cut out a piece of paste roughly the same size as one of the cake sides. Attach it to the cake and trim to size, then cover the opposite side in the same way. Roll out some more blue sugarpaste and cover the bottom of the cake, including the card. Once the bottom is covered, place the cake onto a sheet of parchment or baking paper to prevent it sticking to the work surface. Cover the top of the cake, then the back and front in the same way as for the sides and trim away any excess paste. Run two cake smoothers along the edges of the cake to make neat, sharp corners.

7 Use a dab of royal icing to stick the two legs centrally on the cake board, spacing them slightly apart. Dab a little royal icing on top of each leg, then carefully position the cake on top.

8 Moisten the 20cm (8") long dowel with edible glue then push it through the cake, leaving around 4–8cm (1½–3") protruding from the top to support the head.

NECK

9 Roll a 4cm (1½") thick sausage from 35g (1¼oz) of grey modelling paste, then trim the ends to make it 2cm (¾") in length. Mark two rings

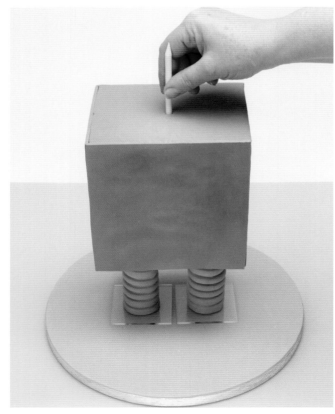

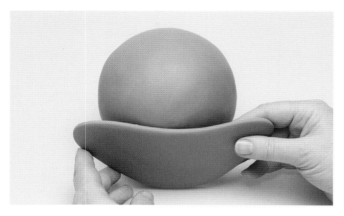

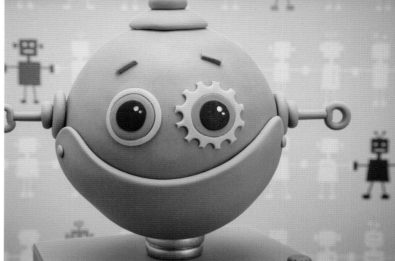

around the paste in the same way as for the legs, then gently push it down the cake dowel.

HEAD

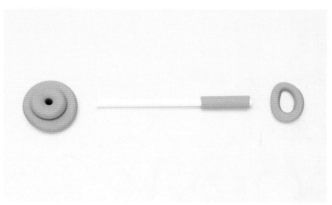

10 Shape 340g (12oz) of marshmallow rice cereal into a ball, then moisten it with a little edible glue. Roll out the remaining blue sugarpaste and cover the ball completely. Smooth around the shape with your hands, stretching out any pleats and closing the join.

11 To make the mouth, roll 45g (1½oz) of blue modelling paste into a tapered sausage shape which is much thicker in the centre, then press down on it with a smoother. Smooth around the edges to neaten, then stick the mouth in place on the bottom half of the head. Immediately push the head into position on the dowelled neck.

12 Moisten the lolly sticks with edible glue, push each stick into a ball of blue sugarpaste and roll it back and forth with a smoother to cover the stick completely. Cut away 4cm (1½") of paste from the bottom of each stick. Cut another 1.5cm (⅝") from the top of the longer lolly stick and no more than 3mm (⅛") from the remaining two sticks. Model flattened circles and dome shapes from blue sugarpaste and assemble on the top and sides of the head, following the picture as a guide. Push the smaller lolly sticks in place on either side of the head, securing with edible glue. Insert the longer lolly stick into the top of the head and secure a small ball of red modelling paste on top.

13 To make the ears, split 5g (just under ¼oz) of blue modelling paste in half, roll each piece into a ball and press down to flatten them. Cut out a circle from the centre of each piece using the tip of the larger piping nozzle. Push in one side to make the circles into D-shapes, then stick in position at the end of each ear and hold for a few moments to secure.

14 For the eyes, use the cutters to cut out small circles from the cream, lilac and black modelling paste. Use a piping nozzle to cut out

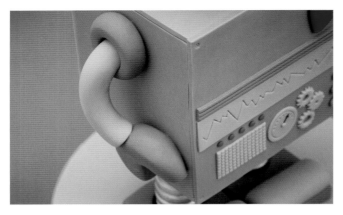
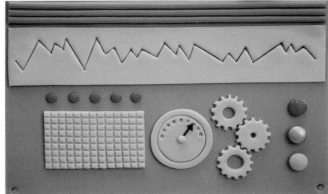

semicircles from around the edge of one of the cream discs to make it look like a cog. Stick the discs to the face one on top of the other.

ARMS

15 For the shoulders, split 60g (2oz) of lilac modelling paste in half, roll each piece into a ball then press down on them with a cake smoother. Cut a 2cm (¾") circle from the centre of each piece and stick the resulting hoops in position on either side of the body.

16 Split 120g (4¼oz) of lilac modelling paste in half and roll each piece into a ball for the hands. Press down on them with a cake smoother, then cut a small wedge from each piece. Stick the hands on the either side of the robot's body, with the cut-out section positioned towards the front of the cake.

17 For the arms, split 75g (2½oz) of grey modelling paste in half and roll each piece into a sausage shape. Bend the paste slightly and secure on each side of the body between the shoulders and hands with a little edible glue.

SHOES

18 Roll out 400g (14oz) of lilac modelling paste to a 2cm (¾") thickness and cut out two rectangles, each measuring 10cm x 7cm (4" x 2¾") in size. Cut out a 3.5cm (1⅜") circle towards the back of the rectangles then cut them open at the back. Pull open the paste so you can slot the feet around the bottom of each leg, then use edible glue to stick the cut edges back together.

19 Roll 120g (4¼oz) of grey modelling paste into a 7cm (2¾") sausage and cut in half lengthways. Stick these in position at the front of each shoe, then attach a tiny ball of grey paste to the end of each piece.

ROBOT CONTROLS

20 For the cogs use the small round cutters to cut out circles from cream modelling paste. Use a piping nozzle to cut circles from the edge and the centre of the paste to make a cog shape.

21 For the heart monitor, roll out a strip of cream modelling paste that will fit across the robot's body and cut the edges straight with a sharp knife. Mark the heartbeat line across the paste with a small knife or cut small pieces of card to the size you require and press the edges neatly into the paste. Roll out a thinner piece of paste the same length as the first and mark three horizontal lines along it with the edge of a ruler. Secure above the first strip of paste.

22 For the grid, cut out a rectangular piece of modelling paste and mark grid lines across it using the edge of a ruler. Stick this below the heart monitor to one side.

23 For the dial, cut out a piece of modelling paste with a small round cutter, then indent a line just inside the edge of the paste with a slightly smaller round cutter. Use the end of a piping nozzle to make marks around the top half of the circle, then model a very small arrow and attach it to the centre of the dial.

24 Model the heart and buttons from any leftover modelling paste and attach to the front of the body with a little edible glue.

FINISHING TOUCHES

25 Mix the silver dust food colour with a little lemon extract (or clear alcohol) until it reaches a paintable consistency. Use no. 3 and no. 4 paintbrushes to paint the silver mixture over the legs and neck, adding a little more lemon essence as it evaporates. Add highlights to the eyes at both one o'clock and two o'clock positions.

26 Trim the edge of the cake board with stripped ribbon to finish (see page 21).

Mini Robot Friends

EDIBLES
(per cake)

5cm x 5cm x 3.5cm (2" x 2" x 1¼") cuboid cake, or 5cm x 6cm x 3.5cm (2 x 2¼" x 1¼") cuboid cake, or two 5cm (2") diameter half-sphere cakes (see recipes on pages 6–9)

20–25g (¾oz) marshmallow rice cereal (see page 11)

45g (1½oz) cake filling (see recipes on pages 10–12)

Lustre dust (powder) food colours: gold and silver (SK)

Edible glue (see page 14)

Sugarpaste in colours of your choice:

    60g (2oz) for body

    30g (1oz) for head

    25g (just over ¾oz) for cake card

Modelling paste (see page 14):

    30g (1oz) in colours of your choice

EQUIPMENT
(per cake)

Basic equipment (see pages 15–17)

10cm (4") square cake card

Lolly stick

Selection of small round cutters

1 Either cut the cakes for the robots' bodies from a larger square cake/traybake or bake individual cakes in miniature cake tins that are the size and shape you require.

2 Cut the cakes into one or two layers then sandwich them together with cake filling. You can leave the robots' bodies square, or trim off the shoulders to make them more rounded. Spread a layer of filling over the surface, then cover the cakes with 60g (2oz) of sugarpaste in your chosen colour (see page 20).

3 Cover a cake card with sugarpaste and place one of the cakes onto it, positioning it towards the back of the card to make space for the legs. Insert a lolly stick into the top of the robot's body and shape a piece of modelling paste around it for the neck.

4 Model the arms, legs or wheels and robot controls from your chosen colours of modelling paste, following the instructions in the main project as a guide. Attach them to the body with edible glue.

5 Model the robots' heads from marshmallow rice cereal mix, then cover each one with 30g (1oz) of sugarpaste in your chosen colour. Add the facial details, ears and antennae following the instructions for the main cake, then position the head on top of the lolly stick.

6 Paint the robot with a mixture of lustre dust food colour and lemon extract (or clear alcohol) to achieve a metallic effect.

TIP

For the robots' heads, simply press down onto the rice cereal mix with a cake smoother and cut out the required shape with a sharp knife.

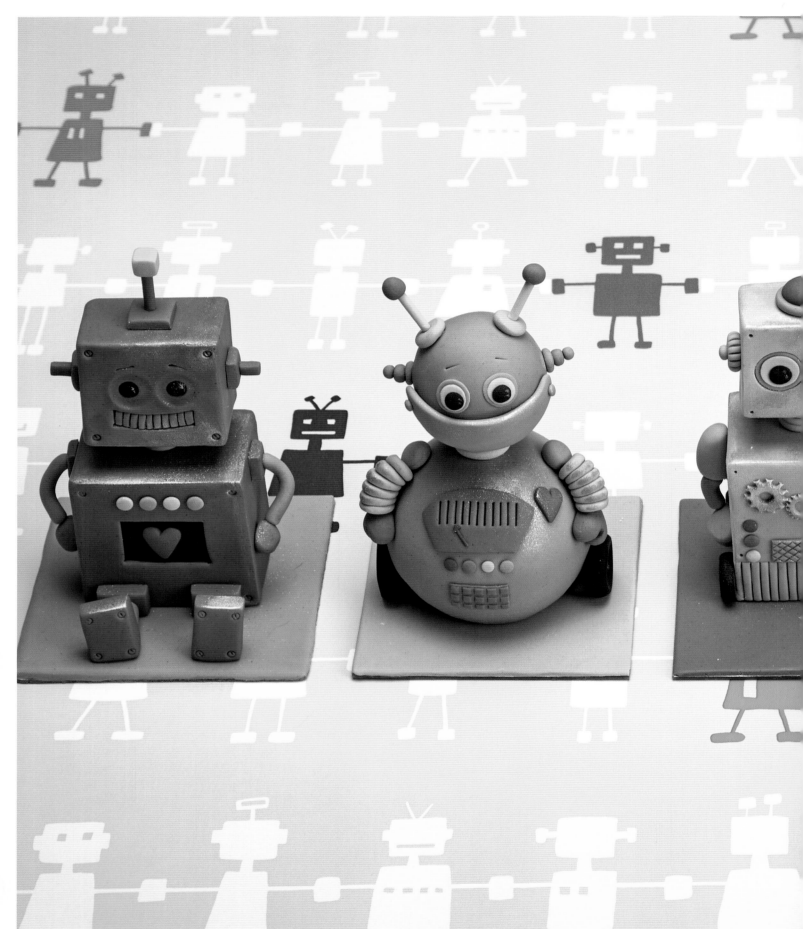

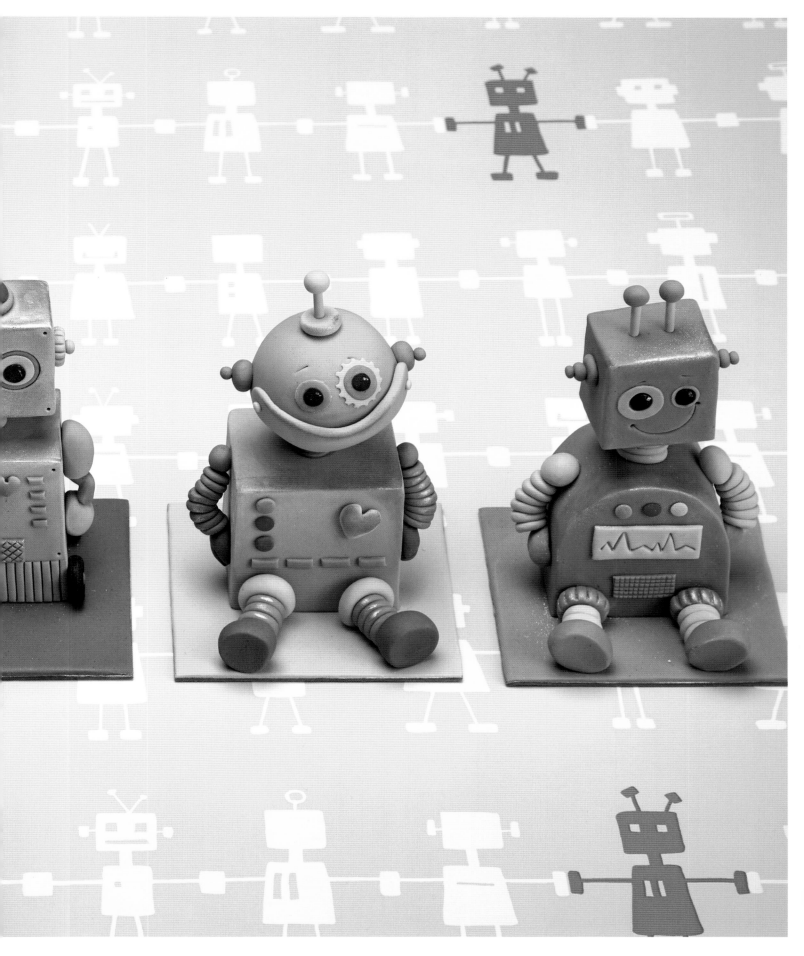

Ahoy Me Hearties!

This fun pirate ship looks impressive balancing on a sea wave. The sea is actually made from a simple cake stand and the cake is secured to it with a large dowel. The royal iced sea foam brings it all nicely together.

EDIBLES

20cm (8") half-sphere or bowl-shaped cake, 6.5cm (2½") deep (see recipes on pages 6–9)

2 x 20cm (8") round cakes, 4cm (1½") deep (see recipes on pages 6–9)

350g (12¼oz) cake filling (see recipes on pages 10–12)

200g (7oz) chocolate ganache or melted white chocolate (see page 12)

115g (4oz) royal icing (see page 13)

Lustre dust (powder) food colour: gold (SK)

Sugarpaste (rolled fondant):

    1.2kg (2lb 10¼oz) golden brown

    650g (1lb 7oz) blue

Modelling paste (see page 14):

    175g (6oz) brown

    150g (5¼oz) black

    65g (2¼oz) golden brown

    45g (1½oz) white

    35g (1¼oz) blue

    35g (1¼oz) red

    25g (just over ¾oz) skin tone

    15g (½oz) grey

    10g (¼oz) lime green

5g (just under ¼oz) green

Pea-sized piece of bright yellow

Tiny piece of pale yellow

EQUIPMENT

Basic equipment (see pages 15–17)

12cm (5") round cake card

20cm (8") round cake board

10cm (4") round polystyrene dummy, 8cm (3") deep

5mm (¼") diameter food-safe dowels: 15cm (6") long, 45.5cm (18") long and sharpened at one end

3mm (⅛") diameter food-safe dowels or wooden barbecue skewers: 18cm, 20cm and 25cm (7", 8" and 10") long

12cm (5") plastic lolly stick

Sugar stick or short length of raw, dried spaghetti

Piping nozzles (tips): nos. 1.5, 18 (PME)

3 x 60cm (24") lengths of strong cream/beige thread

Spare cake dummy of any size, or ball of sugarpaste (to hold the figures whilst modelling)

Templates (see page 149)

CAKE STAND (SEA)

1 Spread a little royal icing over the bottom of the polystyrene dummy and stick it to the cake board so it is slightly off-centre. Cut the round cake card to shape following the base template. Make a small hole in the centre of the card using the tip of a knife then stick the card on top of the cake dummy with royal icing.

> ### TIP
>
> If you prefer, you can make the figures and other items in advance and insert them into a spare cake dummy to hold them upright whilst drying. Store in a cardboard cake box or pop a little cling film (plastic wrap) over each piece to keep them protected.

2 To create the wave effect, first press 100g (3½oz) of blue sugarpaste against the side of the cake dummy and secure with edible glue. Smooth up and down the paste to create a sloped effect.

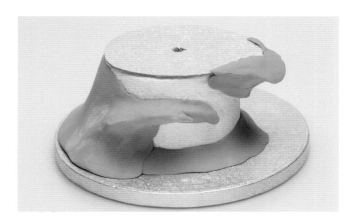

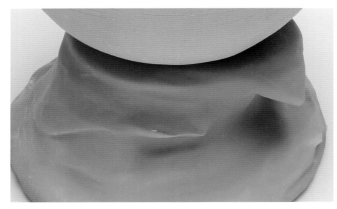

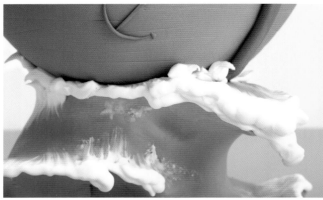

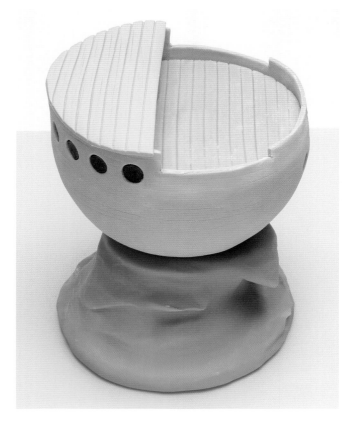

Secure 50g (1¾oz) of blue sugarpaste to the front of the dummy, wrapping the paste around the edge of the protruding cake card. Roll 15g (½oz) of blue sugarpaste into an uneven sausage and stick it halfway up the side of the dummy. To make the sea continue smoothly from the dummy to the board, roll another 45g (1½oz) of blue sugarpaste into a sausage and stick it around the base of the dummy, smoothing the paste up onto the side of the cake dummy and down onto the cake board.

3 To find the dowel hole easily, insert a cocktail stick into the hole in the cake card and push it in at a slight angle so it pierces the polystyrene. Moisten the cake stand and board with a little cooled, boiled water or edible glue. Roll out the remaining blue sugarpaste until it is large enough to cover the cake stand and board entirely, then lift it over the stand so the cocktail stick pokes through and smooth it gently down and around the shape (see page 20).

4 Pinch out waves at the front, along the sides and at the base of the stand. Trim any excess from around the edge of the cake board, making sure the whole board is covered. Remove the cocktail stick and set aside to dry.

CAKE

5 Level the top of the cakes and cut each of them into two layers. Cut an 8cm (3⅛") wide strip from one of the round cakes to create the raised quarterdeck. Stack the round cake on top of the domed cake to make the curved shape of the boat, then place the quarterdeck on top so it sits towards the back of the ship, securing each layer with cake filling. The total height of the cake with the cake filling should be approximately 12–13cm (5"). Spread ganache or melted white chocolate over the surface of the cake to create a crumb-coat (see page 19).

6 Roll out 115g (4oz) of golden-brown sugarpaste and mark planks across the surface using the edge of a ruler. Stick in place over the main deck of the ship using a little edible glue and trim to size with a pair of scissors. Cover either side of the door at the front of the quarterdeck with two rectangles of textured golden-brown sugarpaste, leaving a 3.5cm (1⅜") gap in the centre.

7 Roll out 400g (14oz) of golden-brown sugarpaste and cut out a 15cm x 30cm (6" x 12") rectangle, so it is approximately 2–3cm (¾–1⅛") higher than the cake. Brush a little edible glue over one side of the cake, then dust the sugarpaste with icing sugar and loosely roll up the ends to make it easier to lift. Hold it in position against the cake and unroll the sugarpaste around one side. Cover the opposite side in the same way, so the two pieces meet at the ends of the ship. Gently rub the surface with a ball of sugarpaste trimmings to smooth it, then scratch woodgrain lines into the sugarpaste using a knife.

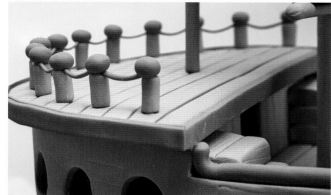

8 Make a 1cm (³/₈") cut down into the sugarpaste in line with the quarterdeck on either side of the cake, then continue to cut a 10cm (4") long strip from the top of the sugarpaste covering. Cut out the portholes and cannon holes from the sides of the ship using the wide end of a piping nozzle. Roll out some black modelling paste into a thin sheet, cut out circles of the same size and use them to fill the holes. Cover the area for the doorway with a thin piece of black modelling paste.

9 To cover the quarterdeck, roll out 90g (3oz) of golden-brown sugarpaste. Cut out a piece slightly larger than the surface area and use a ruler to mark on planks as before. Lay this over the top of the raised cake at the back of the ship. Trim the edge of the quarterdeck with long rectangles of brown modelling paste.

10 To make two sets of stairs, roll out some more golden-brown sugarpaste to 8mm (¼") thick and cut out two 4cm x 5cm (1½" x 2") rectangles, two 3cm x 5cm (1¹/₈" x 2") rectangles and two 2cm x 5cm (¾" x 2") rectangles. Stack three rectangles of each size together then cut down either side with a sharp knife to blend the joins. Mark the stairs with a woodgrain effect and stick on either side of the quarterdeck.

11 To make the ship's mast, roll 30g (1oz) of golden-brown sugarpaste into a long, thin strip, moisten the 45cm (18") dowel with edible glue and gently wrap the paste around it. Roll the dowel on the work surface to close the join and mark a woodgrain effect along the surface (this will also help to disguise the join). Measure from near the base of the stand to the top of the cake then remove that length of sugarpaste from the end of the dowel. Cover the remaining dowels in the same way, trimming 5cm (2") excess from the bottom of the 25cm (10") dowel, then set aside to dry.

12 Roll a long, thin sausage of golden-brown modelling paste and cut it into thirteen 1cm (³/₈") lengths for the railings. Position the railings around the edge of the quarterdeck, top each one with a flattened ball of brown modelling paste then attach very thin sausages of brown paste between them.

13 Split 45g (1½oz) of brown modelling paste in half and roll two 20cm (8") lengths that are fuller at one end and tapered at the other. Press down on each length with a cake smoother to flatten them slightly. Brush edible glue over the fuller end of each piece and roll up slightly to make a small spiral. Position the spiral at the top and stick the lengths down either end of the cake to cover the joins in the sugarpaste. Hook them over a little at the top to prevent them from slipping down. Roll lengths of brown modelling paste and attach them around the top of the ship, curling the ends around. Roll two long, brown lengths and attach them along either side of the ship, so they sit just below the cannons.

14 Hold the 18cm (7") dowel across the 25cm (10") dowel to make a cross shape. Wind the cotton thread around the two dowels, crossing it over to make it stable, then tie securely at the back. Repeat with the 15cm (6") dowel across the 45cm (18") mast, then attach the 20cm (8") dowel 10cm (4") below the first.

15 Make three small swags from 20g (¾oz) of black modelling paste, mark pleats across them with a paintbrush handle and attach them across the smaller mast.

16 Push the main mast centrally down through the cake until it pokes through the underside, then line it up with the hole in the cake stand and push down until only the sugarpaste-covered part of the mast shows. Brush a little edible glue around the base.

TIP

The main mast will anchor the cake to the stand, but to make it even more secure, squeeze a little royal icing directly between the joins.

SEA FOAM

17 For the sea foam effect, pipe a little royal icing at a time along the tip of each wave and around the bottom of the ship. Place a damp paintbrush halfway into the piping and brush outwards to smudge the icing.

TIP

Keep washing and blotting your brush with kitchen paper to make it just damp enough to dissolve the royal icing.

SAILS

18 Roll out the black modelling paste into a thin sheet and cut out the large sail shape using the template. Moisten the ends of the sail with a little edible glue then stick in position between the dowels across the main mast, folding over the top of the sail and holding for a few moments until secure. Insert the smaller mast into the quarterdeck.

CROW'S NEST AND FLAGS

19 For the flags, make two flattened teardrop shapes from black modelling paste. Pinch around the outside edge to give them shape then set the flags aside.

20 Roll the remaining golden-brown modelling paste into a teardrop shape and flatten either end on the work surface. Mark plank lines around the outside with a ruler then make a hole through the centre with a cocktail stick. Place the crow's nest on its side and roll it back and forth to straighten. Push the nest down onto the top of the mast and secure in place with edible glue. Cut out short strips of brown modelling paste and attach them vertically around the sides, then attach a longer strip around the top of the nest.

21 Top each of the masts with a flattened circle and a small ball of brown modelling paste. Moisten the poles with a little edible glue where each flag will sit. Once tacky, press the flags in place and hold for a few moments until secure.

ANCHOR

22 Roll a thin sausage of grey modelling paste for the central shank, round off the end and flatten with a cake smoother. Cut a hole in the rounded end using a no. 18 piping nozzle and stick it to the side of the ship. Roll another very small, thin sausage in the same way but

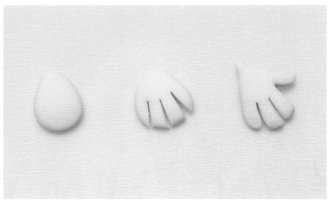

make rings at both ends with a no. 1.5 nozzle and attach across the shank. Roll a third longer, tapered sausage for the hook at the bottom, bend it into a curve and attach to the end of the shank. Add two tiny grey triangles to either end of the hook. Make the chain from tiny rings of grey modelling paste and a small square for the bolt.

PIRATE'S HOOK AND CANNONS

23 To make the pirate's hook, roll a small pea-sized piece of grey modelling paste into a thin sausage with a point at one end. Curl it around into the shape of a question mark then set aside to dry.

24 Split the remaining grey modelling paste in half and roll each piece into a ball for the cannons. Pinch the paste a third of the way from the end to bring out a cone shape then push a small ball tool into the end of the cannon.

PIRATE

Trousers

25 Put aside 5g (just under ¼oz) of blue modelling paste then roll the remaining paste into a ball and flatten it slightly. Squeeze either side to narrow the paste then cut straight across the top. Make another cut down the centre and finish approximately 1cm (³⁄₈") from the top to separate the legs. Smooth down each leg and square off the ends, creating some pleats and folds with the end of a paintbrush.

26 Roll 2g (pinch) of black modelling paste into an oval shape and pinch up one end to make the top of the boot. Roll your finger over the middle of the paste to round off the toe area then stick to the end of one trouser leg with a little edible glue.

27 For the wooden leg, roll a large pea-sized piece of brown modelling paste into a gently tapering sausage and cut the ends

straight. Mark on the woodgrain-effect with a small knife. Push a cocktail stick into the top of the leg then wind it back and forth to open up the hole. Remove the cocktail stick, then glue the wooden leg to the bottom of the trousers. Moisten the lolly stick with a little edible glue and push it up through the wooden leg, into the trouser leg at a slight angle and up through the centre of the trousers. Leave 2.5cm (1") protruding from the bottom of the leg.

Shirt, belt and jacket

28 Roll 20g (¾oz) of white modelling paste into a rounded teardrop and press down on it to flatten slightly. Cut the fuller end straight and stick it in place over the top of the lolly stick, securing at the join with edible glue. Roll out some black modelling paste into a thin sheet, cut it into tiny strips and attach across the white top.

29 Make a slightly thicker strip of black paste for the belt and attach it around his waist. Push the end of a paintbrush into a thin piece of black paste, wind it around to open up the buckle then cut the paste into a small square. Brush the surface with edible gold lustre dust then stick in place.

30 Roll out some red modelling paste into a thin sheet and cut out the pirate's jacket using the template. Wrap the jacket around his torso and secure with edible glue. Add a small strip of red paste for the collar and a tiny rectangle for the back of his jacket. Split another 10g (¼oz) of red modelling paste in half and roll them into sausages for the sleeves. Make an indent in the end of each sleeve with a paintbrush handle.

Hand

31 Roll a large pea-sized piece of skin-tone modelling paste into a teardrop and flatten it slightly. Make a cut in one side for the thumb then make two further cuts to separate the fingers. Smooth each finger to remove any ridges and push the thumb down towards the palm. Roll gently at the wrist area and stick into the end of the sleeve with a little edible glue. Glue the hook into the opposite sleeve.

Head and hat

32 Roll 20g (¾oz) of skin-tone modelling paste into an oval shape for the head. Push a piping nozzle into the face at an angle to mark on the mouth. Add a small ball of skin-tone paste for the nose. Indent the eye area with a ball tool and add one tiny ball of white modelling paste for his eye. Add a tiny oval pupil and a very small piece of black paste for the eyelashes. Model two oval-shaped ears from skin-tone paste, mark the centre of each one with the end of a paintbrush and attach to either side of the head. Roll a tiny ball of skin-tone paste, cut in half and use one half for the eyelid. Make the eye patch from black modelling paste in the same way, but make it slightly larger.

33 For the pirate hat, roll a 5g (just under ¼oz) ball of black modelling paste and flatten it down until it measures approximately 5cm (2") in diameter, then push in either side with your fingers. Stick it in place on his head then turn up the brim and pull both sides down.

34 Model a flattened teardrop shape from brown modelling paste for the beard, pinch up the sides to make the sideburns and cut the end into a point. Stick in position then pull down the mouth area slightly. Use the remaining brown modelling paste to model the hair, eyebrows and moustache. Add a tiny string of black modelling paste across the eyepatch.

Parrot

35 To make the body, roll the lime green modelling paste into a long teardrop then gently stroke the pointed end to bring out the tail. Cut into the end of the tail to make feathers. Moisten the sugar stick or length of raw, dried spaghetti with edible glue then push it down through the neck, leaving 2.5cm (1") protruding from the bottom and a little at the top to support the head.

36 Split the green modelling paste in half, roll into long teardrop shapes and smooth each piece flat. Snip into the pointed end to

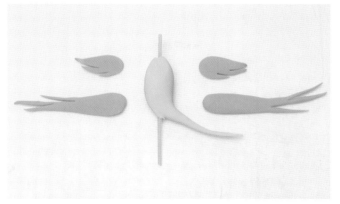

Treasure Map Cupcakes

make feathers and stick on either side of the body. Make two smaller wings with the remaining blue modelling paste. Stick on top of the green wings, positioning them so they stand out from the body. Push the support in the bottom of the parrot into the front of the ship and secure with a little edible glue.

37 Set aside a tiny piece from 5g (just under ¼oz) of red modelling paste then roll the remaining paste into a small ball, squeezing the top to narrow it slightly. Attach two pale yellow ovals for the eyes, then add smaller blue and black ovals on top. Add small red pieces of paste above for the eyelids.

38 For the beak, roll the bright yellow modelling paste into a teardrop and push a knife in just under the pointed end to mark on the mouth. Pinch out the tip of the beak and turn it down slightly. Indent the corners of the mouth with the tip of a cocktail stick. Make a hat in the same way as for the pirate using 2g (pinch) of black modelling paste and secure in place with edible glue.

SKULL AND CROSSBONES

39 Thinly roll out some white modelling paste then cut out the skull and crossed swords using the picture as a guide. Cut out the eyes and nose area with piping nozzles and shape with the end of a paintbrush or cocktail stick. Cut tiny strips of white modelling paste for the teeth, stick in place then cut through to separate the teeth. Stick the skull and swords design centrally on the sail.

40 Following the picture as a guide, cut out the skull and crossbones design for the pirate's hat from a thin sheet of white modelling paste and attach it to the brim of the hat. Repeat for the parrot's hat.

EDIBLES
(per cupcake)

Cupcake baked in blue cupcake case (see recipes on pages 6–9)

20g (¾oz) cake filling (see recipes on pages 10–12)

Sugarpaste (rolled fondant):
  30g (1oz) dark cream

Modelling paste (see page 14):
  20g (½oz) pale cream
  10g (¼oz) grey

Paste food colours: blue, brown, green and golden-brown (SK)

Lustre dust (powder) food colours: gold and silver (SK)

EQUIPMENT
(per cupcake)

Basic equipment (see pages 15–17)

Teddy bear texture mat (SK)

Round cutter: 8cm (3⅛")

Piping nozzle (tip): no. 18 (PME)

Thin plastic lolly stick

1 Bake as many cupcakes as required then spread some cake filling over the top. Cut out a circle of dark cream sugarpaste, push a texture mat into the surface and place on top of the cupcake.

2 Roll out two thirds of the pale cream modelling paste into a thin sheet and cut out a 5cm x 8cm (2" x 3⅛") rectangle. Cut around the edge of the paste to make it look like torn paper. Roll up either end slightly and secure to the cupcake with edible glue. Dilute the paste colours with a little cooled, boiled water and use a fine paintbrush to paint on the map. Rub a little gold lustre dust around the edge.

3 For the coins, press the texture mat over the surface of some more pale cream modelling paste and cut out circles using a no. 18 piping nozzle. Brush some gold lustre dust over the surface.

4 For the sword, roll the grey modelling paste into a long, tapering sausage and flatten. Stroke the opposite sides to flatten them further and create a ridge down the centre. Brush silver lustre dust over the surface. Roll a large pea-sized piece of pale cream modelling paste into a sausage shape, round off the ends and stick it onto the wider end of the blade.

5 Cut the blade in half and push a small lolly stick into the wider end, leaving a little protruding. Wrap a long, thin sausage of pale cream modelling paste around the lolly stick. Add a loop of paste and a small ball for the handle and brush with gold lustre dust. Leave to dry before inserting both pieces into the cake and remove before eating.

Pirate Cupcakes

EDIBLES
(per cupcake)

Cupcake baked in blue cupcake case (see recipes on pags 6–9)

20g (¾oz) cake filling (see recipes on pages 10–12)

Sugarpaste (rolled fondant):

   20g (¾oz) skin tone

   10g (¼oz) red

   Small piece of black and white

Dust (powder) food colour: red (SK)

EQUIPMENT
(per cupcake)

Basic equipment (see pages 15–17)

Piping nozzle (tip): no. 18 (PME)

Round cutters: 4cm and 8cm (1½" and 3")

1 Bake as many cupcakes as required then spread some cake filling over the top.

2 Cut out a circle of skin-tone sugarpaste and place on top of the cupcake. Smooth the surface with a small ball of trimmings. Indent a smile using the 4cm (1½") cutter and add dimples with the end of a paintbrush. Make an oval-shaped nose and two ears from the skin-tone sugarpaste.

3 Cut out a semicircle of red sugarpaste with the 8cm (3⅛") cutter and stick to the top of the cupcake. Roll the red trimmings into teardrop shapes for the ties behind the ear. Cut out several white spots with a no. 18 piping nozzle and stick over the headscarf.

4 Make a black oval for the eye, a larger black triangle for the eyepatch and a thin, black sausage for the string. Brush the cheeks with red dust food colour to finish.

Safari Friends

The eyes of my baby grandson, Liam, widened with delight when he saw this cake – he thought it was a new toy he could play with! Lions, elephants and giraffes are always popular with children and although it looks impressive, this cake is surprisingly straightforward to make.

EDIBLES

2 x 15cm (6") half-sphere or bowl-shaped cakes, each 8cm (3") deep (see recipes on pages 6–9)

2 x 7cm (2½") half-sphere cakes, each 3.5cm (1⅜") deep (see recipes on pages 6–9)

400g (14oz) cake filling (see recipes on pages 10–12)

200g (7oz) chocolate ganache or melted white chocolate (see page 12)

250g (8¾oz) marshmallow rice cereal (see page 11)

Edible glue (see page 14)

Dust (powder) food colour: pink (SK)

2 x 3cm (1⅛") long yellow sugar sticks (see page 14)

Sugarpaste (rolled fondant):
    1.27kg (2lb 13oz) light grey
    370g (13oz) bright green
    330g (11½oz) golden-brown

    185g (6½oz) yellow

    45g (1½oz) dark golden-brown

    15g (½oz) light brown

    5g (just under ¼oz) white

Modelling paste (see page 14):
    595g (1lb 5oz) dark green
    140g (5oz) light grey
    10g (¼oz) black

EQUIPMENT

Basic equipment (see pages 15–17)

35cm (14") round cake board

3 food-safe cake dowels: 12cm, 20cm and 30cm (5", 8" and 12") long

3 x 6cm (2⅜") long lolly sticks

Round cutter: 4cm (1½")

Small piece of folded card

1.15m x 15mm width (46" x ⅝") ribbon: zebra print

CAKE BOARD

1 Cover the cake board with bright green sugarpaste (see page 21). Smooth over the surface with a cake smoother then press a large rolling pin into the paste to create ripples. Trim any excess paste from around the edge and set aside to dry.

MARSHMALLOW RICE CEREAL HEADS

2 To make the elephant's head, shape 115g (4oz) of marshmallow rice cereal into a rounded teardrop and press it between your hands until it's compacted and firm. Split 5g (just under ¼oz) of marshmallow rice cereal in half and use it to pad out the cheeks. Press down on the top of the head to make an indent in the centre.

3 For the giraffe and lion, use 45g (1½oz) of marshmallow rice cereal for each head and model them into teardrop shapes. Use the remaining marshmallow rice cereal to make an oval shape for the giraffe's muzzle and a larger oval for the lion's muzzle and rounded cheeks. Press them firmly in place on the heads and set aside.

TIP

This cake will give you the standard 20 small servings but if you need more, simply scale up the size of the elephant's body by using two 18cm or 20cm (7" or 8") half-sphere cakes instead.

CAKES

4 Level the top of the cakes and cut each of them into two layers. Sandwich the layers together with cake filling to make one large ball and one small ball. Spread a layer of ganache or melted white chocolate over the surface of each cake, then set the smaller cake aside.

ELEPHANT

Body

5 Moisten the larger cake with a little cooled, boiled water or edible glue, then use 75g (2½oz) of light grey sugarpaste to pad out the neck area on top of the cake.

6 Roll out 595g (1lb 5oz) of light grey sugarpaste and cover the cake completely, smoothing down and around the shape (see page 20). Trim any excess from around the base and smooth the edge under the cake to round it off. Rub the surface of the cake with a ball of sugarpaste trimmings to remove any dimples. Stroke your fingers across the surface of the cake to create wrinkles in the skin.

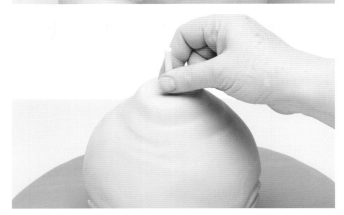

7 Position the cake towards the back of the cake board, securing with a little edible glue. Push the 20cm (8") dowel down through the neck area and into the cake, leaving approximately 3cm (1⅛") protruding from the top.

Legs

8 Split 260g (9oz) of light grey sugarpaste in half for the back legs. Roll your fingers back and forth over the centre of the paste to stretch it out and round off one end for the foot, leaving the thigh slightly fuller. Stick the legs up against the elephant's body using edible glue then smooth over the join until it has blended into the surface completely.

> **TIP**
>
> If the paste you are using is very stretchy and difficult to blend, moisten your fingers with a little water to make it easier.

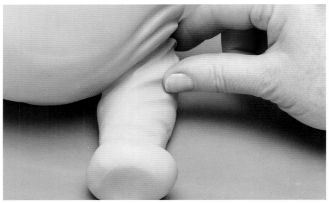

9 Split 175g (6oz) of light grey sugarpaste in half to make the front legs. Model the paste in the same way as for the back legs but round off the centre to make the knees. Stick in place at the shoulders, blending the join as before. For the toes, add four balls of light grey sugarpaste to the end of each foot. Make the two toes in the centre of each foot slightly larger and pinch along the top to shape.

Head

10 Roll out 140g (5oz) of light grey sugarpaste and cover the elephant's marshmallow rice cereal head, smoothing around the shape and tucking any excess paste underneath. Indent two eye sockets using a ball or bone tool. Moisten a lolly stick with edible glue and insert it into the face, leaving half protruding ready to support the trunk.

11 For the trunk, roll 60g (2oz) of light grey modelling paste into a long teardrop then roll out the narrow end until it is approximately 8cm (3") in length. Push the handle of a paintbrush into the narrower end of the trunk to open up the snout, then pinch the end of the snout to shape it. Cut the wider end of the trunk flat then secure over the lolly stick and blend in the join. Roll a paintbrush handle over the surface to create wrinkles, then push the end of the handle into the face to make two dimples.

12 For the eyes, model two small, flattened circles of white sugarpaste and secure them in the eye sockets. Position two smaller circles of black modelling paste on top and add tiny balls of white paste at the one o'clock position. Add a very small piece of black paste over each eye for the eyelashes then roll two tiny eyebrows from leftover grey sugarpaste.

13 Push the head down onto the dowel in the cake and secure to the body with edible glue. Roll three small, pointed teardrops from light grey sugarpaste and secure them to the top of the elephant's head to make a tuft of hair.

Ears

14 Push the two remaining lolly sticks into either side of the elephant's head, ready to support each ear. Split the remaining light grey modelling paste in half, then roll one half into a teardrop shape. Roll it out with a rolling pin to flatten it, keeping the side that will sit against the elephant's head a little thicker. Roll the rolling pin over the outside edge to thin and frill the paste. Fold over the top a little then stick in place over the lolly sticks, blending the join at the top. Smooth the ear backwards and stroke the paste with your fingertips to make wrinkles. Make and attach the opposite ear in the same way, then brush a little pink dust food colour over the cheeks and ears.

Tail

15 Roll the remaining light grey sugarpaste into a tapered sausage for the tail. Roll a small teardrop of black modelling paste, make two snips in the tip and secure to the end of the tail. Attach to the back of the elephant so the black end is resting on the cake board.

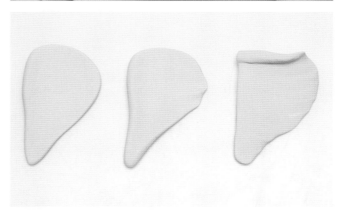

GIRAFFE'S NECK

16 Push the 30cm (12") dowel down into the back of the elephant's body, just behind the right shoulder, until it reaches the cake board. Roll 90g (3oz) of yellow sugarpaste into a 12cm (5") long teardrop and cut off the tip. Using a little edible glue to secure, push the rounded end down over the dowel. Smooth down behind the shoulder and cover the dowel completely. For the spots, roll several different-sized balls of dark golden-brown sugarpaste, flatten them out and stick them randomly over the giraffe's neck.

BUSHES

17 Split the dark green modelling paste into five pieces that graduate in size. For a tall bush, roll a piece of paste into an oval shape then roll it out with a rolling pin, keeping the shape and making the bottom thicker than the top. Make the round bushes in the same way, but start with a ball instead of an oval. Push a folded piece of card into the outside edge of each bush to give it shape then rub the surface of the paste with a cake smoother. Flatten the base of each bush to help it stand up. Stick the two largest bushes around the giraffe to support it, then arrange the others on the cake board and secure with a little edible glue.

GIRAFFE'S HEAD

18 Set aside 10g (¼oz) of yellow sugarpaste and use the remainder to cover the giraffe's head, smoothing around the shape and tucking any excess paste underneath. Indent the eye sockets with a ball or bone tool and use a 4cm (1½") round cutter to make the mouth. Use the end of a paintbrush to add dimples and push the smaller end of a ball or bone tool into the muzzle to make nostrils. Make the eyes and eyebrows as for the elephant. Add dark golden-brown spots around the back of the head in the same way as the body. For the ears, roll two small teardrop shapes from yellow sugarpaste then make an indent in the centre of each one. Push the yellow sugar sticks into the top of the head and top with two small balls of yellow sugarpaste. Push the head onto the neck and secure with a little edible glue.

LION

19 Moisten the surface of the smaller cake with a little cooled, boiled water or edible glue. Roll out 115g (4oz) of golden-brown sugarpaste and cover the cake completely, smoothing around the shape. Push the excess paste upwards to make the body into a teardrop shape and bring out the neck. Run a paintbrush handle over the surface of the paste to create a fur effect. Push the 12cm

(5") dowel down into the body, leaving a little protruding to support the head.

20 Roll out 90g (3oz) of golden-brown sugarpaste, cover the head in the same way as for the elephant and indent eye sockets with a bone or ball tool. Roll out the light brown sugarpaste into an oval shape, stick it over the muzzle area and pinch out the chin. Indent a mouth in the same way as for the giraffe and mark a line up to where the nose will sit with the back of a knife. Make the eyes and eyebrows as for the elephant and add a little oval of black modelling paste for the nose. Roll two large pea-sized balls for the ears and make an indent in the centre of each one with a bone or ball tool. Push the head onto the neck and secure with a little edible glue.

21 For the paws, split 35g (1¼oz) of golden-brown sugarpaste into four equal pieces and roll each one into an oval. Make two indents in the front of each paw with the back of a knife. Split another 35g (1¼oz) of golden-brown sugarpaste in half and roll the pieces into rounded teardrop shapes for the back legs. Split 45g (1½oz) of the same paste in half and roll into long, flattened teardrop shapes for the front legs. Attach the legs to the body with a little edible glue, then secure a paw to the bottom of each leg. Roll the remaining golden-brown sugarpaste into a long tail, stick it in place on the back of the lion so it is standing up and curl the end over. Hold in place for a few moments until secure.

22 Roll a piece of dark golden-brown sugarpaste for the mane, pinch up the paste to make it spiky and attach around his face to frame it. Make a beard in the same way and attach it under the chin. Roll a teardrop for the end of the tail, make two snips in the tip and secure in place.

23 Trim the edge of the cake board with zebra print ribbon to finish (see page 21).

Safari Friends Mini Cakes

EDIBLES
(per cake)

2 x 7cm (2½") half-sphere cakes (see recipes on pages 6–9)

30g (1oz) cake filling (see recipes on pages 10–12)

65g (2¼oz) marshmallow rice cereal (see page 11)

Dust (powder) food colour: pink (SK)

Sugarpaste (rolled fondant):

Zebra

325g (11¼oz) white

45g (1½oz) black

20g (¾oz) grey

Hippo

310g (10¾oz) light grey

25g (just over ¾oz) pink

A little black and white

Tiger

310g (10¾oz) golden brown

60g (2oz) white

10g (¼oz) black

5g (just under ¼oz) pink

Rhino

310g (10¾oz) dark grey

5g (just under ¼oz) black

5g (just under ¼oz) white

EQUIPMENT
(per cake)

Basic equipment (see pages 15–17)

10cm (4") round cake card (optional)

Round cutter: 5cm (2")

A lolly stick

1   Sandwich the half-sphere cakes together with a little cake filling, then spread more filling over the surface of the cake. Cover each cake with sugarpaste in your chosen colour then insert a dowel down into the top, leaving a little protruding to support the head.

ZEBRA

2   Model the marshmallow rice cereal into the same shape as for the giraffe's head. Split 25g (just over ¾oz) of white sugarpaste into four pieces and roll into sausages for the legs, tapering each slightly at one end. Add a small ball of black paste for the hooves and press down to flatten slightly.

3   Cover the zebra's head in the same way as the giraffe and add a grey muzzle in the same way as for the lion, marking on the mouth with a 5cm (2") round cutter. Brush pink dust food colour over the muzzle. Model two white, teardrop-shaped ears and roll the end of a paintbrush back and forth in the centre of each one. Stick them in place, flattening the fuller end against the head.

4   For the mane, roll a 5g (just under ¼oz) long teardrop of white sugarpaste, flatten it down and smooth around the edge. Cut a straight edge along one side and thicken that edge slightly. Make lots of cuts along the opposite side, cutting out small V-shapes randomly. Stick the mane down the back of the zebra's head. Make a white tail in the same way as for the hippo, adding a teardrop of black paste for the tip. Add black stripes in the same way as for the tiger, bringing some of the stripes up the sides of the mane.

HIPPO

5 Model the marshmallow rice cereal into the same shape as the giraffe's head. Shape the hippo's body in the same way as for the lion, adding wrinkles with the end of a paintbrush. Make the legs in the same way as for the elephant using light grey sugarpaste. Roll small pea-sized pieces of light grey paste, press them down and cut in half. Stick these semicircles across the top of each foot for the toes.

6 Cover the hippo's head with light grey sugarpaste and mark on the mouth with a 5cm (2") round cutter. Cut out a 5cm (2") circle of rolled-out pink paste, smooth the edge and stick over the muzzle. Make the mouth and nostrils as for the giraffe and add two tiny squares of white paste for the teeth.

7 Add two pea-sized balls for the ears in the same way as for the lion. Roll 5g (just under ¼oz) of light grey sugarpaste into a tiny

tapering tail and add a teardrop of black paste for the tip, cutting into it twice with a knife. Brush pink dust food colour over his body, adding a little more over the tummy area.

TIGER

8 Model the marshmallow rice cereal into the same shape as the lion's head. Pinch out the neck at the top of the cake to make a teardrop shape then make the front legs and back legs in the same way as for the lion, but with white paws.

9 Roll a white teardrop for the tummy patch, press down to flatten it and smooth around the edge with your fingertips. Secure the white paste to the tiger's tummy, then attach the legs. Roll an 8cm (3") long tail from golden-brown sugarpaste then stick it against the tiger's back and press on the end to round it off. For the stripes, roll small pieces of black sugarpaste that are no larger than a small pea. Taper

the ends, press down to flatten and attach over the tiger's body, legs and tail.

10 Cover the tiger's head with golden-brown sugarpaste, then cover the muzzle with white sugarpaste and attach more black stripes. Pinch gently at the bottom to bring out the chin, then make the mouth in the same way as for the lion. Add an oval of pink sugarpaste for the nose, place your finger across the top then use the end of a paintbrush to make nostrils. Make the eyes, eyebrows and ears in the same way as for the lion. Brush the cheeks with pink dust food colour.

RHINO

11 Model the marshmallow rice cereal into the same shape as the giraffe's head. Shape the rhino's body in the same way as for the lion, adding wrinkles with the end of a paintbrush. Make the legs from dark grey sugarpaste in the same way as for the elephant. Attach small,

tapering sausages of dark grey paste across the top of the front legs to make wrinkles. Make the toes in the same way as for the hippo.

12 Cover the rhino's head in the same way as the giraffe's and mark the mouth in the same way, using a 5cm (2") round cutter. Push your finger into the top of the muzzle to make an indent for the large horn. Roll 5g (just under ¼oz) of dark grey paste into a pointed teardrop for the large horn, curling it upwards slightly. Secure a second pea-sized horn just above the first. Brush pink dust food colour over the cheeks.

13 Add two teardrop-shaped ears, making them in the same way as for the zebra. Make a tiny tapering tail using 5g (just under ¼oz) of dark grey paste and roll a paintbrush handle over it to create wrinkles. Add a black teardrop at the tip, cutting into it twice with a knife.

Ladybird Toadstool House

I love the gravity-defying cakes that are popular now and was inspired to create this toadstool cake. It's exceptionally easy and uses a simple stand to elevate the cake.

EDIBLES

10cm, 15cm and 20cm (4", 6" and 8") round cakes, 7.5cm (3") deep (see recipes on pages 6–9)

400g (14oz) cake filling (see recipes on pages 10–12)

200g (7oz) chocolate ganache or melted white chocolate (see page 12)

Edible glue (see page 14)

Dust (powder) food colouring: red (SK)

30g (1oz) white royal icing (see page 13)

Sugarpaste (rolled fondant):

   1kg (2lb 3¼oz) cream

   550g (1lb 3½oz) red

   20g (¾oz) beige

Modelling paste (see page 14):

   110g (3¾oz) black

   25g (just over ¾oz) red

   20g (¾oz) green

   10g (¼oz) soft beige

   10g (¼oz) pale cream

   Pinch of white

EQUIPMENT

Basic equipment (see pages 15–17)

Cake supports:

   30cm (12") diameter round wooden base board with central hole, 23cm (9") long threaded dowel and 10cm (4") diameter wooden support disc with central hole (see page 18) *or* 18cm (7") high x 10cm (4") diameter acrylic cake separator and 30cm (12") cake drum

18cm (7") round cake card

Small piece of card

Round cutters: 2cm, 2.5cm and 3cm (¾", 1" and 1¼")

3 x 5cm (2") sugar sticks or lengths of raw, dried spaghetti

Small plastic lolly stick

Piping nozzle (tip): no. 18 (PME)

1m x 15mm width (39" x ⅝") satin ribbon: green spotty

Important note: If you are using an MDF cake stand, make sure the cake is placed on a food-safe cake card so no edible part touches the MDF. Although the cake sits above the threaded dowel, you can always cover this with food-safe cake board foil and slip a hollow plastic dowel over it if you prefer. Use royal icing to attach the cake board foil. Alternatively, you could use an 18cm (7") high acrylic stand on a regular cake board instead.

CAKE BOARD

1 Cover the base board with 315g (11oz) of cream sugarpaste (see page 21) and cut out the paste covering the central hole. Smooth the surface with a cake smoother then press a rolling pin over the board to create ripples. If you're using an acrylic stand, cut a small circle in the centre of the rolled-out paste and cut a line to the edge of the paste to open up the circle. Lift and position the sugarpaste on the board, wrapping it around the stand, then smooth over the join.

CAKES

2 Level the top of the cakes and cut each of them into two layers. Place the largest cake on a cake card then stack the smaller cakes on top. Use a large serrated knife to cut down from the top of the cake at an angle to create sloping sides and remove the top edges. Keep trimming until you have a neat, smooth surface. Trim around the bottom so it curves inwards to meet the edge of the cake card underneath.

3 Sandwich all the layers together with cake filling then spread a layer of ganache or melted white chocolate over the surface of the cake as a crumb-coat (see page 19).

STALK

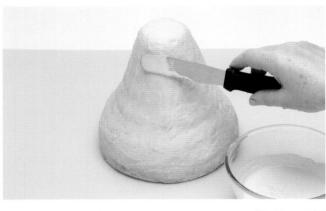

4 Screw the 23cm (9") central dowel into the threaded hole in the base board. The base board is 3cm (1⅛") deep, so once the support disc is on top this will make the stalk approximately 18cm (7") tall. If you're using a normal cake drum with a thinner acrylic stand then the stand will only need to be 18cm (7") in height.

5 Roll 300g (10½oz) of cream sugarpaste into a sausage that is the same length as the threaded dowel. Moisten the length of the dowel with edible glue then push the sausage of paste around it to cover it completely. Squeeze the paste halfway up the dowel to narrow it slightly.

TIP

Gravity will drag the paste down so keep stroking it upwards.

6 Wind the support disc down onto the threaded dowel until it is level with the top. Smooth the sugarpaste up onto it and secure with edible glue. Rub the surface of the stalk in a circular motion with a small ball of sugarpaste trimmings to remove any dimples.

7 Stick the cake on its board to the support disc using royal icing and leave to dry.

DOOR AND WINDOW

8 Cut out a 5cm x 3.5cm (2" x 1⅜") rectangle from a piece of card then round off the top to make a template for the door. Push the template into the sugarpaste at the base of the stalk, smoothing over the surface and around the outside edge. Push a 2.5cm (1") round cutter into the paste just above the doorway to indent the window and run your fingertips over the paste inside the circle to make it deeper. Fill the window with a 2cm (¾") circle of beige sugarpaste.

9 Cut out a door from green modelling paste using the template as a guide, then mark lines down it with the edge of a ruler. Add a tiny ball of green paste for the door handle and use a knife to scratch a woodgrain effect into the door. Secure the door in place with edible glue. Roll several different-sized ovals from beige sugarpaste, flatten them down and stick them over the cake board in front of the door to make the pathway.

10 To make the window frame, roll some green modelling paste into a thin sheet, cut out a 2.5cm (1") circle then cut out a 2cm (¾") circle from the centre to make a hoop. Attach the hoop over the indented paste and secure two little strips of green paste across the window.

TOADSTOOL

11 Stick a small sausage of paste around the support disc and smooth the paste up onto the bottom of the cake card. Make four 6cm wide x 8cm long (2½" x 3") teardrop shapes using 60g (2oz) of cream sugarpaste for each one, then make four more teardrops of the same length but slightly thinner using only 30g (1oz) each. Press down on each teardrop to flatten it and smooth around the shape, making the largest four thicker around the outside edge. Stick the teardrops to the underside of the cake with royal icing, butting them up closely against each other.

12 Moisten the surface of the cake with a little cooled, boiled water or edible glue. Roll out the red sugarpaste and use it to cover the cake completely (see page 20), smoothing down and around the shape. Trim the excess paste neatly from around the base, leaving a little overlapping the bottom edge of the cake. Rub a ball of sugarpaste trimmings over the surface of the cake to remove any dimples.

13 For the spots, cut out thin circles of cream sugarpaste with the different-sized cutters and attach over the top of the cake with edible glue. Use flattened balls of cream sugarpaste for the smaller spots.

14 To make the chimney, roll a small amount of pale cream modelling paste into a sausage that is thicker at one end and bend it in half. Push the thicker end of the paste against the side of the cake to flatten the area where you will attach it and cut the top straight. Roll the remaining green modelling paste into a teardrop shape and flatten the fuller end. Push a plastic lolly stick into the flattened area of the toadstool, leaving some protruding from the cake. Push the chimney onto it and secure at the base with edible glue. Stick the green roof in place once the chimney is secure.

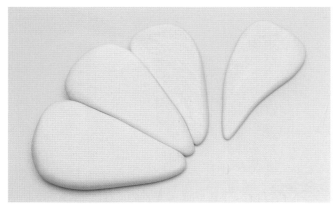

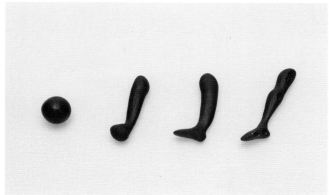

LADYBIRDS

15 For the antennae, split a small pea-sized ball of black modelling paste into six pieces and roll each piece back and forth between your fingertips, rounding off one end. Set all aside to dry.

TIP

Make the antennae first to allow for drying time.

16 For the body, split 20g (¾oz) of black modelling paste into four pieces that graduate in size. Roll the three smallest pieces into balls and press down to flatten them slightly. Stick them one on top of the other, with the smallest piece at the bottom. Roll the fourth piece into a ball and press down on it, smoothing the sides to make a dome shape. Stick this on top of the other pieces and push a sugar stick or length of raw, dried spaghetti down into the body, leaving a little protruding at the top to support the head. Secure in place with edible glue. Repeat for the remaining two ladybirds.

17 Split 30g (1oz) of black modelling paste into three pieces and roll into balls for the heads. Squeeze either side of the top of each ball to indent them slightly, then stick them in place with a little edible glue. For the eye area, roll a large pea-sized piece of soft beige modelling paste into a sausage, make an indent in the centre and round off both ends. Turn each end upwards then press down with a cake smoother and attach to the front of the head. Make the mouth area in the same way, but keep it rounded and pinch out a small chin.

18 Push a piping nozzle into the mouth area at an angle to create a smile and use a cocktail stick to add dimples. Add a tiny oval of soft beige modelling paste for the nose. Make two oval-shaped indents in the eye area using the small end of a bone tool and fill with tiny ovals of white modelling paste. Attach two ovals of black modelling paste for the pupils and use two more tiny pieces for the eyelashes. Dust the cheeks with red dust food colouring.

19 Split 10g (¼oz) of black modelling paste into twelve small pieces for the legs. Roll each piece into a sausage and round off one end. Squeeze the rounded end to lengthen it then bend it around, pinching out a heel at the back. Hold the middle of the leg between your fingers and roll back and forth to narrow the paste, then bend into position. Attach four legs to each ladybird with a little edible glue, holding them in position for a few seconds to secure.

20 Roll out the red modelling paste to a thickness of 5mm (just under ¼") and cut out three circles using the 3.5cm (1⅜") round cutter. Smooth around the outside edge to make them dome-shaped then cut them in half. Stick to the back of a ladybird and add some black spots. Use a cocktail stick to make a hole in either side of each head for the antennae and carefully stick these in place with a tiny amount of edible glue. Avoid using too much edible glue as this will soften the paste and the antennae may droop.

21 Position the ladybirds on the cake board and secure with a little edible glue.

RIBBON

22 Trim the cake board with the green spotty ribbon to finish (see page 21).

Ladybird Cupcakes

EDIBLES
(per cupcake)

Cupcake baked in white cupcake case (see recipes on pages 6–9)

20g (¾oz) cake filling (see recipes on pages 10–12)

Sugarpaste (rolled fondant):

    20g (¾oz) green

    15g (½oz) white

    Pinch of yellow

Modelling paste (see page 14):

    10g (¼oz) black

    5g (just under ¼oz) red

    Pinch of soft beige

EQUIPMENT
(per cupcake)

Basic equipment (see pages 15–17)

8cm (3") round cutter

8cm (3") daisy cutter

1 Bake as many cupcakes as required then spread cake filling over the top in a dome shape.

2 Cut out a circle from green sugarpaste and a daisy from white sugarpaste then place in position on the top of each cupcake. Roll some yellow sugarpaste into a ball, flatten it down and stick it in the centre of each one.

3 To make a mini ladybird, model smaller versions of the body, wings, front legs, head and antennae from black, red and soft beige modelling paste. Secure to the top of the cupcake.

Ladybird Mini Cakes

EDIBLES
(per cake)

7cm (2¾") diameter half-sphere cake (see recipes on pages 6–9)

20g (¾oz) cake filling (see recipes on pages 10–12)

Dust (powder) food colour: red (SK)

Sugarpaste (rolled fondant):

    75g (2½oz) black

    15g (½oz) red

    10g (¼oz) soft beige

    Pinch of white

Modelling paste (see page 14):

    Pinch of black (for antennae)

EQUIPMENT
(per cake)

Basic equipment (see pages 15–17)

A lolly stick

Round cutters: 1.5cm and 8cm (⅝" and 3")

1 Level the top of the cake slightly but keep the rounded edge. Cut the cake into two layers, sandwich them together with cake filling then spread a little over the surface. Thinly roll out the black sugarpaste and cover the cake completely, smoothing around the sides and underneath.

2 Roll out the red sugarpaste and cut out a circle using the 8cm (3") round cutter. Smooth around the outside edge and stick in place on top of the cake. Mark a line down the centre with the back of a knife and decorate with black spots.

3 Insert a lolly stick into the cake to support the head. Roll a 30g (1oz) ball of black sugarpaste for the head, gently push it onto the lolly stick and secure with edible glue.

4 Make the front legs, antennae and facial features in the same way as for the main cake, but use a 1.5cm (⅝") round cutter to mark on the mouth. Indent the corners of the mouth with a cocktail stick then push the end of a paintbrush into the mouth to pull down the bottom lip. Add a tiny piece of white modelling paste to each eye at the one o'clock position (or use a tiny dot of white paste food colour). Dust the cheeks with red dust food colour to finish.

Choo-Choo Train

I wanted to include a train design in this book as they are always popular with small children. I decided he had to be bright red and aqua blue with a cute, smiling face and a little puff of steam to make it look like he is chugging along quite happily!

EDIBLES

2 x 20cm (8") square cakes, 4cm (1½") deep (see recipe on pages 6–9)

350g (12¼oz) cake filling (see recipes on pages 10–12)

200g (7oz) chocolate ganache or melted white chocolate (see page 12)

Edible glue (see page 14)

Sugarpaste (rolled fondant):

    650g (1lb 7oz) aqua

    400g (14oz) red

    375g (13¼oz) pale aqua

    200g (7oz) black

    10g (¼oz) white

Modelling paste (see page 14):

    90g (3oz) aqua

    50g (1¾oz) red

EQUIPMENT

Basic equipment (see pages 15–17)

30cm (12") round cake board

4 x 14cm (5½") paper lolly sticks

Food-safe cake dowel: 15cm (6")

Round cutters: 2.5cm, 3cm, 5cm, 7.5cm and 9cm (1", 1⅛", 2", 3" and 3½")

Piping nozzle (tip): no. 1.5 (PME)

6cm (2⅜") square cake card

Small piece of folded card

Template (see page 149)

1.02m x 15mm width (40" x ⅝") satin ribbon: aqua

CAKE BOARD

1 Cover the cake board with 315g (11oz) of pale aqua sugarpaste (see page 21).

CAKE

2 Trim the crusts from both cakes and slice the tops flat. Cut both cakes in half lengthways to make four 20cm x 10cm (8" x 4") rectangular cakes. Stack two together to make the base of the engine and set aside.

3 Stack the remaining two rectangles one on top of the other and cut in half again to make four square cakes. Set two of these squares aside for the cab then carefully carve the remaining cakes into a cylinder to form the rounded engine. As you are carving the cake, form a rounded teardrop shape at the front for the face.

4 Cut layers in each of the three cake parts then sandwich them back together with cake filling, saving some cake filling for later.

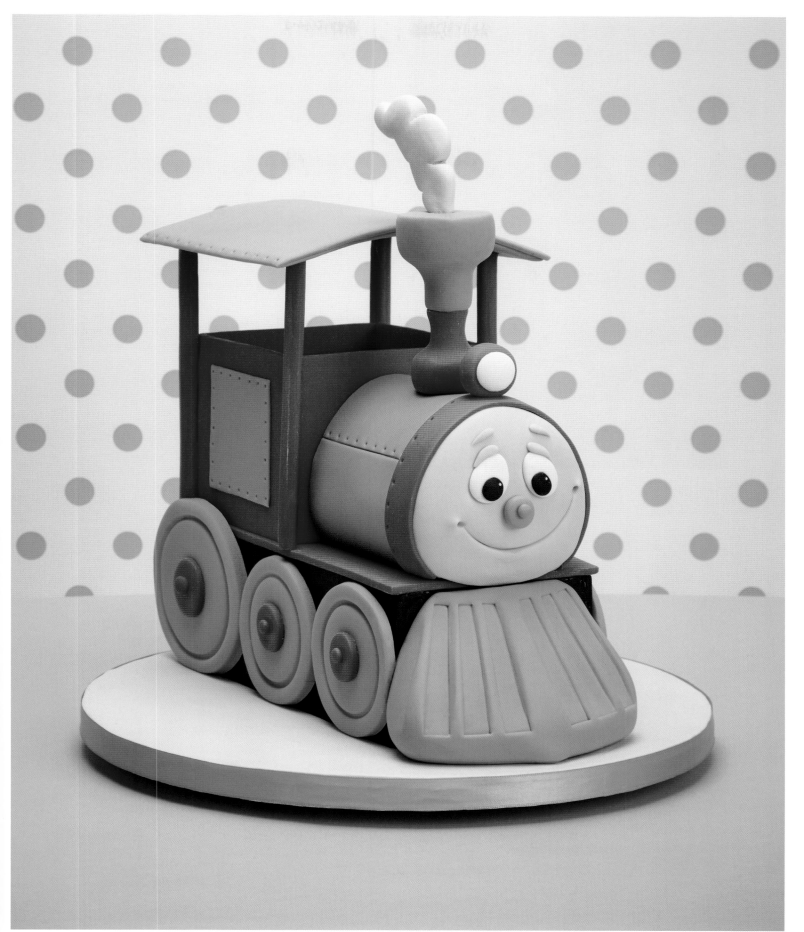

Spread a layer of ganache or melted white chocolate over the surface of all the cakes as a crumb coat. Keep the three cakes separate for now.

TRAIN BASE

5   Measure the height of the rectangular cake. Using this measurement, roll out 160g (5½oz) of black sugarpaste and cut a strip to this width and measuring 60cm (24") in length to cover the four sides. Lift the paste and position it around the cake sides, pressing into place with smoothers and trimming neatly at the join. Alternatively, you can cover each side separately and smooth the corner joins closed if you find this easier.

6   Carefully lift the covered cake by pressing on either side with cake smoothers and place on the cake board slightly towards the back. Roll out 145g (5oz) of red sugarpaste, cut a piece slightly larger than the top of the cake and place it in position. Press a cake smoother along the edge in case to ensure it is straight.

CAB

7   Thinly roll out approximately 30g (1oz) of black sugarpaste, moisten the top of the square cake with edible glue then turn it over and place the glued side down on the rolled paste. Cut around the shape. While the cake is still upside down on the paste, spread a little cake filling on the top of the cake, turn it over and position at the back of the covered rectangular cake, leaving room for the engine at the front.

8   Moisten the sides of the square cake with a little edible glue. Roll out 180g (6¼oz) of red sugarpaste and cut four 10cm x 11.5cm (4" x 4½") pieces to cover all four sides separately, each one being 1.5cm (⅝") higher than the sides of the cake. Mark lines along the sides of the paste to resemble wooden planks by running the back of the knife horizontally over the surface.

9   To make the roof supports, roll a sausage of red sugarpaste to the same length as a lolly stick, then moisten a lolly stick with edible glue and press the stick down onto the paste until it sinks in. Pinch the paste up around it to close the join then roll back and forth to smooth the surface. Press down with a cake smoother then turn and repeat on the side to square off the edges. Cut away any excess sugarpaste from the top and bottom. Mark a wooden effect with the back of a knife as before. Repeat for the remaining three supports then stick them in position against each corner of the square cake.

ROOF

10 Bend the 6cm (2³/₈") square cake card into a curve and brush the curved underside with edible glue. Thinly roll out 75g (2½oz) of aqua sugarpaste and use this to cover the underside of the card, trimming away any excess from around the edge with a sharp knife. Cover the top with another 75g (2½oz) of aqua sugarpaste and smooth with a cake smoother. Indent rivets along opposite sides of the roof using the tip of a piping nozzle.

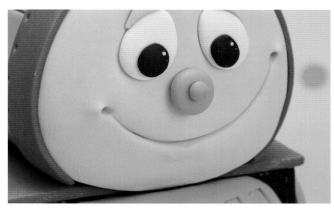

ENGINE

11 Roll out 100g (3½oz) of aqua sugarpaste and cut a strip to cover the rounded sides of the engine, leaving the face uncovered. Mark a seam on either side with a ruler, then indent rivets along the seam as before. Stick the engine on the cake using a little cake filling where it joins onto the cab.

12 To make the face slightly dome-shaped, roll 60g (2oz) of pale aqua sugarpaste into a ball, press down and smooth the surface until it spreads out and is thinner around the outside edge. Push up the edges slightly at the top to create a slight teardrop shape. Stick the paste onto the front of the engine, using a little edible glue around the outside edge to secure it in place.

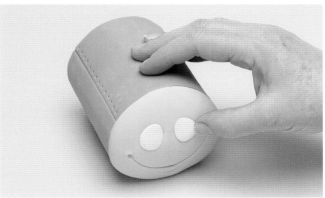

13 Mark the smile with the 7.5cm (3") round cutter then smooth along the line with your finger from the edges towards the centre, pushing down slightly to create a bottom lip. Indent dimples using the handle of a paintbrush.

14 Mark two eyes by pressing into the paste with your index finger. Add two flattened ovals of white sugarpaste followed by round pupils made from black sugarpaste and a tiny white highlight on each eye at the one o'clock position.

15 Use the pale aqua sugarpaste trimmings to make small sausages for the eyelids and eyebrows and stick them in place with edible glue. Model a nose from a ball of aqua sugarpaste as shown and attach it to the centre of the face.

16 Roll out 15g (½oz) of red sugarpaste into a thin sheet and cut a strip to frame the face. Wrap it around the engine, trim to size and indent rivets as before. For the light above his face, roll a 10g (¼oz) ball of red modelling paste and press down to flatten it slightly. Add a white domed circle to the front and stick the light upright to the top of the engine.

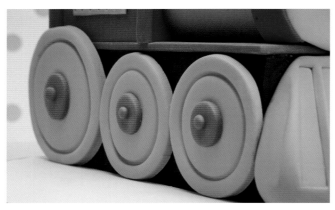

17 For the base of the funnel, roll the remaining red modelling paste into a ball and roll this back and forth, pressing halfway down the paste to narrow the top. Stick it in position on top of the engine and push a cake dowel down through the centre, leaving around 7.5cm (3") protruding from the top.

WHEELS

18 Roll out some aqua sugarpaste and cut two large circles and four smaller circles using the 9cm (3½") and 7.5cm (3") round cutters. Indent a rim into each wheel using the 7.5cm (3") round cutter for the larger wheels and the 5cm (2") for the smaller ones. Roll out some red sugarpaste and cut two 3cm (1⅛") circles and four 2.5cm (1") circles for the wheels. Stick them in place with edible glue then add a small ball onto the centre of each.

FINISHING TOUCHES

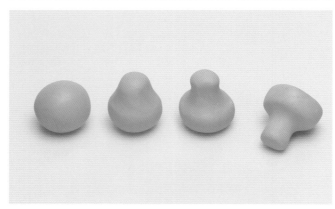

19 Thinly roll out the aqua modelling paste and cut out three 6cm (2⅜") squares and secure them to the sides of the cab. Indent rivets along the edges as before. Stick the roof in position with edible glue, holding for a few moments until secure.

20 Model the top part of the funnel using 30g (1oz) of aqua modelling paste, shaping it in the same way as the base. Push it into place over the dowel.

21 Mix together the white and black sugarpaste trimmings to make grey. Roll it into a long teardrop shape and press down with a cake smoother to flatten it slightly. Push a small piece of folded card around the outside edges to create a cloud shape then stick in position on top of the funnel, supported by the top of the dowel.

22 To make the cowcatcher for the front of the train, roll the remaining aqua sugarpaste into a ball and press down using a cake smoother to make a wedge that is thicker at one end and thinner at the other. Push on both sides with the cake smoother to straighten them then press again on top, angling the cake smoother so the paste becomes thicker in the centre. Using the handle of a paintbrush, press the card template into the surface three times on each side and smooth along the lines with your finger. Stick the cowcatcher in position on the front of the engine.

23 Trim the edge of the cake board with aqua ribbon to finish (see page 21).

Runaway Train Cupcakes

EDIBLES
(per cupcake)

Cupcake baked in white cupcake case (see recipes on pages 6–9)

20g (¾oz) cake filling (see recipes on pages 10–12)

Sugarpaste (rolled fondant):

    20g (¾oz) pale aqua

    5g (just under ¼oz) brown

    Pinch of grey

Mini train

    20g (¾oz) pale aqua

    10g (¼oz) aqua

    5g (just under ¼oz) red

    Pinch of black

    Pinch of white

EQUIPMENT
(per cupcake)

Basic equipment (see pages 15–17)

Round cutter (to fit cupcake once shaped with cake filling)

1   Bake as many cupcakes as required then spread cake filling over the top in a dome shape.

2   Cut out a circle of pale aqua sugarpaste to go on each cupcake and place in position. Cut several strips of brown sugarpaste for the sleepers and stick them to the top with edible glue. Roll two long, thin sausages of grey paste for the tracks and secure along both sides of the sleepers.

3   To make a mini train, model simplified versions of the base, wheels, cab and engine from aqua, pale aqua and red sugarpaste using the main cake as a guide. Add the face using tiny amounts of white and black sugarpaste for the eyes and make a little buffer for the front of the train instead of the cowcatcher. Attach the train to the tracks using edible glue.

Cheeky Monkeys

Sometimes it's best to keep it simple and these two little monkeys playing on a tree stump make for an extremely cute cake. This design will certainly delight your own cheeky monkeys and the figures can easily be removed and kept as a memento of the special day.

EDIBLES

2 x 20cm (8") round cakes, 4cm (1½") deep (or 1 x 20cm (8") round cake, 8cm (3") deep) (see recipes on pages 6–9)

350g (12¼oz) cake filling (see recipes on pages 10–12)

200g (7oz) chocolate ganache or melted white chocolate (see page 12)

270g (9½oz) marshmallow rice cereal (see page 11)

Edible glue (see page 14)

Liquid food colour: brown (SK)

Sugarpaste (rolled fondant):

    850g (1lb 14oz) brown

    370g (13oz) green

    345g (just over 12oz) cream

Modelling paste (see page 14):

    325g (11¼oz) brown

    135g (4¾oz) cream

    30g (1oz) dark green

    25g (just over ¼oz) pale pink

    Pinch of black

EQUIPMENT

Basic equipment (see pages 15–17)

35cm (14") round cake board

20cm (8") round cake card

4 food-safe cake dowels

2 lolly sticks

1.15m x 15mm width (46" x ⅝") satin ribbon: dark green

TIP

If the marshmallow mixture is very sticky, leave it to cool down a little more. If it's still too sticky to handle, rub a little butter or oil onto your hands.

CAKE BOARD

1 Cover the cake board with green sugarpaste (see page 21) and set aside.

MARSHMALLOW RICE CEREAL HEADS AND BODIES

2 Roll 75g (2½oz) of marshmallow rice cereal into a teardrop shape for the body and press down on the front to push out the tummy area. Make a second body in the same way.

3 Roll two balls of marshmallow rice cereal for the heads, each weighing 45g (1½oz). To pad out the muzzle area, use the remaining marshmallow rice cereal to make one large ball and two smaller balls for each head. Press the larger ball firmly onto the front of the head and add the two smaller balls on either side for the cheeks.

CAKE

4 Use a large serrated knife to level the top of each cake and trim the crust from around the edges. Cut each cake into two layers, then sandwich all the layers together with cake filling. Stick the cake onto the cake card with a dab of filling. Use a knife to make small notches of different sizes in the top edge of the cake. Spread a layer of ganache or melted white chocolate over the surface of the cake as a crumb-coat (see page 19). Roll out 185g (6½oz) of cream sugarpaste and cover the top of the cake only, shaping the paste around the notches. Press a paintbrush handle into each notch to make an indent.

5 Split 260g (9oz) of brown sugarpaste into six pieces that are roughly the same size. Space them evenly around the base of the cake to pad out the roots, then smooth the paste up onto the surface of the cake. Pinch the ends then twist and taper each piece.

6 Moisten the sides of the cake with a little cooled, boiled water or edible glue. Roll out 400g (14oz) of brown sugarpaste into a thin sheet, then cut out a rectangle that is 70cm (28") long and 1cm (³/₈") taller than the sides of the cake. Dust with icing sugar and carefully roll up the paste. Hold the end of the paste against the cake and unroll it around the sides, securing the join with a little edible glue. Pinch around the top of the paste to give it texture and thin out the edge. Trim any excess from around the base. Shape the sugarpaste around the roots, squeezing each root to give texture and shape. Use the back of a knife to create a woodgrain-effect around the tree stump. Position the cake on the cake board and secure with a little edible glue.

7 Use a fine paintbrush and brown liquid food colour to paint tree rings over the top of the cake.

8 For the tufts of grass, split the dark green modelling paste into six different-sized pieces. Roll each piece into a teardrop shape and make several snips in the tip of each piece using fine scissors. Slice off the base then stick the grass in position around the roots.

MONKEYS

Body

9 Roll 50g (1¾oz) of brown sugarpaste into a teardrop then flatten it out with a rolling pin until it is 2–3mm (¹/₁₆–¹/₈") thick. Use the paste to cover one of the marshmallow rice cereal bodies, covering the back first and smoothing around the sides so the join is at the front (this will be covered by paste later). Cover the second body in the same way.

10 Roll 30g (1oz) of cream sugarpaste into a teardrop and roll out as before. Stick it in position over the front of the monkey's body,

smoothing around the shape to neaten it and bring out a rounded belly. Use the end of a paintbrush to mark on a belly button and smooth a little line underneath. Push the dowel down through the monkey's body, leaving 4cm (1½") at the top. Repeat for the second monkey.

Feet

11 Split 100g (3½oz) of cream modelling paste into four equal pieces then roll one piece into a 5cm (2") long sausage. Make a cut in one end for the big toe, then pull out the paste and round it off. Smooth over the rest of the toe area to flatten it, then cut the paste at an angle to remove the excess. Cut into the paste to make three more toes, then separate and round off each one as before. Pinch around the middle of the foot to narrow it and round off the heel. Make another three feet in the same way and set aside to dry.

Hands

12 Split the remaining cream modelling paste into four equal pieces. Roll one piece into a rounded teardrop then press down on it to flatten it slightly. Make a cut in one side for the thumb, cutting halfway into the hand, then pull the thumb down out of the way. Make two more cuts in the top to separate the fingers then pinch and round off. Push the hand into the wrist area to flatten it slightly then set aside. Make another three hands in the same way.

Legs

13 Divide 135g (4¾oz) of brown modelling paste into four equal pieces, then roll each piece into a tapered sausage that is 8cm (3") long. Pinch the paste halfway along each sausage to make a knee then push in behind the knee to bend the leg. Stick the legs in position on the cake, following the main picture as a guide. Attach the feet with edible glue.

14 Insert a dowel into the top of each of the kneeling monkey's legs, leaving a little protruding from each one. Push the kneeling monkey's body down onto the dowelled legs, then stick the other monkey's body in front so they support each other.

Arms

15 Split 75g (2½oz) of brown modelling paste into four equal pieces, then roll each piece into a 7cm (2¾") long sausage. Pinch halfway along each sausage to bring out the elbow and bend the arm. Stick in position and secure a hand to the end of each arm.

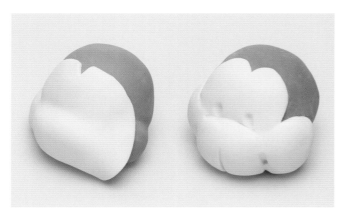

Head

16 Roll out 45g (1½oz) of brown sugarpaste into a circle that is large enough to cover the back of the head. Secure over the back of the head, then smooth the edge of the paste flush with the marshmallow rice cereal.

17 For the face, split the remaining cream sugarpaste in half then roll out one half into a large circle. Secure over the facial area, pulling the edges around the cheeks and tucking the paste underneath the muzzle. Smooth over the facial area to define the contours, then cut a small V-shape into the forehead and above either cheek.

18 Mark a line down the centre of the muzzle using the back of a knife then use the end of a paintbrush to mark on the mouth and dimples. Mark two oval shapes for the eyes and very lightly indent two eyebrows high on the forehead. Push the head down onto the dowel sticking out of the body, securing at the neck with a little edible glue.

19 Repeat steps 16–18 for the second monkey, using the remaining brown and cream sugarpaste.

Ears

20 Push a lolly stick horizontally through each monkey's head near the top, leaving a little protruding on either side to support the ears. Split 60g (2oz) of brown modelling paste into four equal pieces and roll them into balls. Press down on each ball with a cake smoother then push the ears onto the lolly sticks, securing with a little edible glue. Split 10g (¼oz) of pale pink modelling paste into four equal pieces, roll them into balls and flatten with a cake smoother. Secure inside the ears.

Finishing touches

21 Roll two small ovals of pale pink modelling paste for the noses and secure to the top of each muzzle. Roll the remaining pink sugarpaste into an oval, mark a line down the centre with the back of a knife and stick it to the bottom of the kneeling monkey.

22 Model pea-sized amounts of brown modelling paste into teardrop shapes for the hair and position on top of the head. Split the remaining brown modelling paste into two pieces for the tails and roll them into long sausages that are slightly thicker at the ends. Stick one to the back of each monkey and curl them around.

23 Roll very small ovals of black modelling paste for the eyes and secure them in place, slightly tilting them inwards at the top.

24 Trim the edge of the cake board with dark green ribbon to finish (see page 21).

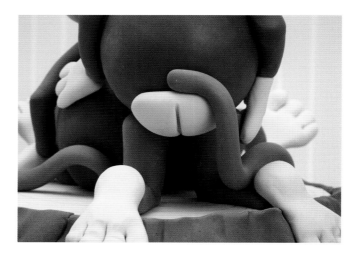

Monkey Cupcakes

EDIBLES
(per cupcake)

Cupcake baked in white cupcake case (see recipes on pages 6–9)

30g (1oz) cake filling (see recipes on pages 10–12)

Sugarpaste (rolled fondant):

25g (just over ¾oz) cream

25g (just over ¾oz) light brown

A little black and pink

EQUIPMENT
(per cupcake)

Basic equipment (see pages 15–17)

1 Bake as many cupcakes as required. Spread cake filling over the lower half of each cupcake to pad out the muzzle and cheeks.

2 Roll out the cream sugarpaste into a circle, cut a V-shape in the top and the sides then cover the top of the cupcake. Shape the paste around the cake filling to make the muzzle.

3 Make the facial features, ears and hair in the same way as for the main cake. Stick the ears in position and support until dry.

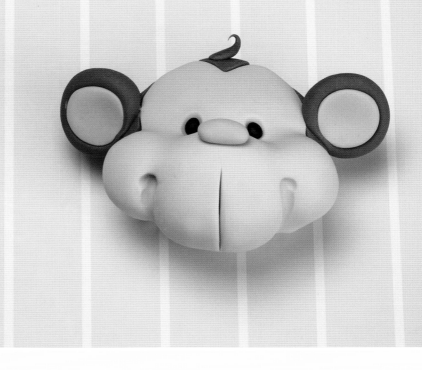

Unicorn Castle

As unicorns are always popular with little girls, I've transformed the traditional fairy-tale castle into a unicorn castle, complete with stable doors and horseshoes. By using a simple cake stand, this enchanting castle cake is seemingly elevated into the clouds, making it feel even more magical.

EDIBLES

2 x 15cm (6") round cakes, 5cm (2") deep (see recipes on pages 6–9)

2 x 10cm (4") round cakes, 5cm (2") deep (see recipes on pages 6–9)

350g (12¼oz) cake filling (see recipes on pages 10–12)

200g (7oz) chocolate ganache or melted white chocolate (see page 12)

Edible glue (see page 14)

Dust (powder) food colour: pink (SK)

Edible sparkle dust (powder): silver

Paste food colour: black (SK)

30g (1oz) royal icing (see page 13)

Sugarpaste (rolled fondant):

    945g (2lb 1¼oz) pale pink

    595g (1lb 5oz) green

    285g (10oz) rose pink

Modelling paste (see page 14):

    200g (7oz) pale pink

    35g (1¼oz) dark pink

    10g (¼oz) white

    5g (just under ¼oz) dark grey

    A little black

EQUIPMENT

Basic equipment (see pages 15–17)

30cm (12") round cake board

Acrylic cake separator: 10cm high x 3cm diameter (4" x 1¼") tube with 7cm (2¾") diameter round top and base

Round cake cards: 2 x 10cm (4") and 1 x 15cm (6")

Spare cake board larger than 20cm (8"), or small non-stick board

6 food-safe cake dowels

Square cutter: 1.5cm (½")

Round cutter: 2cm (¾")

Small rose leaf cutter and veiner (SK)

Small paper lolly stick

Piping nozzle (tip): no. 1.5 (PME)

1m x 15mm (40" x ⅝") sheer ribbon: green sparkly

CAKE BOARD AND STAND

1 Spread royal icing over the bottom of the acrylic cake separator and stick it to the centre of the cake board. Roll out 315g (11oz) of green sugarpaste into a circle large enough to cover the cake board. Moisten the cake board and the base of stand with a little cooled, boiled water or edible glue. Make a cut from the centre to the edge of the sugarpaste, open up the paste and place it around the cake stand and over the board, smoothing the join closed at the back of the board. Smooth over the surface with a cake smoother to help remove the ridge made by the stand. Press a rolling pin over the surface to create ripples and trim any excess paste from around the edge.

> ### TIP
>
> If you'd prefer not to elevate the cake, you can construct the cake in the same way but place it directly on the cake board instead, omitting the acrylic separator.

2 Roll out a thin layer of green sugarpaste and wrap it around the central tube of the acrylic separator. Cover the underside and the edge of the top disc in the same way. Don't worry if the covering looks messy as it will be covered with vines.

3 Roll out several thin sausages of green sugarpaste that are each approximately 30cm (12") long. Brush edible glue over the covered parts of the stand and start wrapping individual vines around the bottom of the central tube. Continue to wind the paste around the tube until it is completely covered.

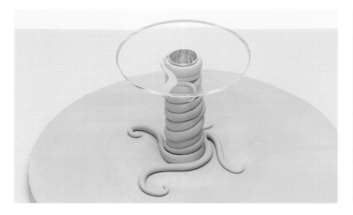

4 Roll out a thin sheet of green sugarpaste and cut out several leaves with the cutter. Dust each one with icing sugar then press them into the leaf veiner. Remove the leaf, twist it to give it some shape and attach to the vines. Set aside some green sugarpaste to make a few more vines once the castle is in position.

CAKES

5 Trim off the crusts and level the top of each cake. Cut each cake into two layers and sandwich them together with cake filling. Assemble the two 10cm (4") cakes on top of each other and place on a 10cm (4") cake card. Assemble the two 15cm (6") cakes in the same way but keep separate from the 10cm (4") cakes for now. Spread ganache or melted white chocolate over the surface of each cake. To achieve a sharp edge, coat the sides of the cake first then cover the top of the cake separately to give the sides time to firm.

6 Brush a little edible glue over the surface of the 15cm (6") cake. Roll out 360g (12½oz) of pale pink sugarpaste and cut out a strip that is 50cm (20") long and the same height as the side of the cake. Dust the surface with icing sugar and roll up the paste from one end. Place the end of the paste against the side of the cake and unroll it carefully, making sure the top edge is in line with the top of the cake. Trim any excess from the join and secure with a little edible glue. Press two cake smoothers around the sides of the cake to achieve a smooth surface.

7 To achieve a neat, even edge around the top of the cake, roll out 115g (4oz) of pale pink sugarpaste and place it over the top of the larger cake. Holding a spare cake board or small non-stick board on top, flip the cake upside down. Trim the excess paste from around the edge then flip the cake back up the right way.

TIP

If the sugarpaste you are using can be rolled out thinly without becoming translucent, you can cover the cakes all in one go and use cake smoothers to achieve a straight top edge.

8 Cover the smaller cake in the same way using 225g (8oz) of pale pink sugarpaste for both the sides and top. The strip of paste for the sides will need to be 35cm (14") long.

9 Cut away an 8cm (3⅛") square of sugarpaste from the front of the 15cm (6") cake to leave a gap for the stable door. Roll out some rose pink sugarpaste into a thin sheet and cut out an 8cm (3⅛") square. Use the edge of a ruler to mark a deep cross into the paste, then use a small knife to mark on wooden planks and create a woodgrain effect. Trim the paste to size again then stick in place at the front of the cake. Make two loops from thin sausages of rose pink paste and attach them to the door.

10 For the shutters, cut out two 1.5cm x 3cm (⅝" x 1⅛") rectangles from the rolled-out rose pink sugarpaste, mark lines down them in the same way as for the door and set aside.

11 Cut out a 3cm (1⅛") square of sugarpaste from the front of the smaller cake. Roll out the dark grey modelling paste, cut out a square the same size and fill in the gap to make the window. Secure a length of pale pink modelling paste across the top of the stable door and a shorter piece under the window, then mark on a woodgrain effect. Roll two pea-sized sausages of paste, bend them around to make horseshoe shapes and make small indents around each one with a piping nozzle. Secure them above the window and door.

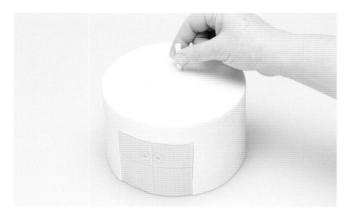

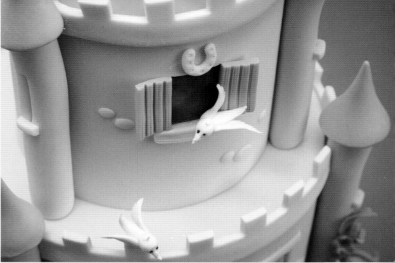

TIP

I have added the turrets after the battlements so they turn out slightly at the top for a cartoony effect. If you would like the turrets to be straight, simply make the battlements afterwards and cut them into smaller lengths so they fit in between.

12   Roll tiny ovals of pale pink sugarpaste, flatten them down and secure randomly over the surface of the cakes to give texture and hide any imperfections, if necessary. Attach the shutters to either side of the window.

13   Dowel both the top and bottom tiers (see page 21), then stick the top tier to the bottom tier with a little royal icing.

ROOF

14   Roll 185g (6½oz) of rose pink sugarpaste into a ball and stick it in the centre of a 10cm (4") cake card. Press the cake smoother around the ball at an angle to make a pyramid shape. Pull the sugarpaste down to the edge of the board whilst keeping a point at the top. Make a flattened teardrop of pale pink modelling paste for the flag and twist the tip to give it movement. Secure to the very top of the roof and top with a tiny, flattened ball of pale pink paste. Stick the cake card onto the top tier using a little royal icing.

BATTLEMENTS

15   Roll out 65g (2¼oz) of pale pink modelling paste and cut out a strip that is 2.5cm (1") deep and as long as the circumference of the top tier cake. Use a cutter to cut out squares from the top of the paste to make the battlements. Moisten the top edge of the cake with a little edible glue then carefully attach the paste around the cake and secure the join at the back. Repeat to make the battlements for the bottom tier: it is best to make one piece at a time so the paste doesn't dry out.

TURRETS

16   Split 120g (4¼oz) of pale pink sugarpaste into three equal pieces then roll them into sausages that are slightly longer than the height of the 15cm (6") cake. Roll a cake smoother back and forth over each piece to achieve a smooth surface. Cut the top and bottom straight and stick two against the cake on either side of the stable door and one centrally at the back. Make three turrets for the top tier in the same way, using 100g (3½oz) of pale pink sugarpaste. Push the end of a ruler lengthways into the middle of each turret to indent arrow slits, adding a tiny pale pink windowsill at the bottom of each one.

17   Divide the remaining rose pink sugarpaste into four equal pieces for the rooftops. Roll the paste into teardrop shapes and press the rounded end on the work surface to flatten it. Smooth down the sides and stick in place on top of each turret, holding for a few moments to secure.

BIRDS

18   Reserve a pea-sized piece of white modelling paste, then roll another two large pea-sized pieces into teardrop shapes with long pointed ends. Make two cuts into the end of each point to separate the feathers. Roll two slightly smaller teardrop shapes then cut into the pointed ends to open up the beaks. Brush with edible glue then sprinkle with edible sparkle dust. Roll four tiny balls from black

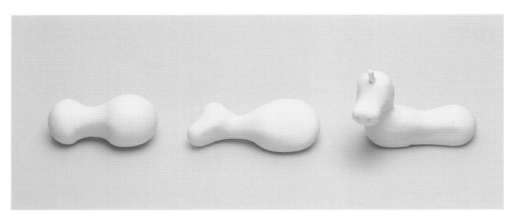

modelling paste and attach them to the heads as eyes. Make another four small teardrop shapes for the wings, flatten them down and cut along the bottom edge to bring out the feathers. Secure the wings to the bodies, then stick the birds in position on the cake.

FINISHING TOUCHES

19   Spread the top of the cake separator with royal icing and carefully position the cake on top. Make some more vines in the same way as before and position them so they spiral up around the base of the cake.

20   For the individual flowers, roll a pea-sized ball of dark pink modelling paste, push the end of a paintbrush into the middle and make five cuts evenly around the bottom. Remove the paintbrush and pinch out each petal. Push the paintbrush handle back into the centre to re-shape it. Brush the base of each flower with edible glue and push into position on a vine.

UNICORN

21   Roll 90g (3oz) of pale pink modelling paste into a ball then roll your fingers back and forth from the centre to one end, so one end is larger than the other. Pinch out a muzzle from the smaller end and round it off. Twist up the neck and carefully insert a paper lolly stick, moistened with a little edible glue, into the forehead and down into the neck for support.

22   Push a small round cutter into the muzzle at an angle to make the mouth. Add dimples in the corners using the end of a paintbrush, then push the paintbrush into the top of the muzzle to open up each nostril. Gently press a ball or bone tool into either side of the face to make the eye sockets.

23   For the legs, split 35g (1¼oz) of pale pink modelling paste into four equal pieces then roll each piece into a long, tapering sausage.

Roll the paste back and forth at the narrower end to round off the hoof and press it flat at the bottom. Roll your finger back and forth just above the middle of the leg to round off the knee, then bend and pinch out the paste. Leave one leg straight. Once you have made a leg, stick it to the unicorn's body and smooth over the paste at the top of the leg to hide the join. Round off the thigh on each back leg.

24   Roll a long, pointed teardrop for the horn and roll a knife over the surface to texture it. Moisten the end of the lolly stick protruding from the head and push the horn carefully in place, holding for a few moments to secure.

25   For the ears, split a pea-sized piece of pale pink modelling paste in half and roll the ends of each piece back and forth between your fingers to narrow them. Press a paintbrush handle into the centre of each ear then stick them in place on the head, smoothing over the join at the front.

26   Add pea-sized pieces of dark pink modelling paste to the bottom of each leg to make the hooves, pressing each flat at the bottom. Roll a long, tapering teardrop for the mane, twist it around and curl up the end. Cut into the fuller end with scissors, stick it down the back of the neck then curl up the fringe. Roll the remaining dark pink modelling paste into a long teardrop shape for the tail, twisting gently as before.

27   Make two tiny, flattened balls of white modelling paste for the eyes. Attach smaller flattened balls of green and black modelling paste for the iris and pupil. Dilute black paste food colour with a little cooled, boiled water and use a fine paintbrush to paint small lines over each iris. Flatten a tiny ball of pale pink modelling paste, cut in half and use to make the eyelids. Roll tiny pieces of black modelling paste for the eyelashes, or paint them on if you prefer. Dust the unicorn's cheeks with pink dust food colour and add edible sparkles to the horn. Secure the unicorn to the front of the cake board.

28   Trim the cake board with green sparkly ribbon to finish (see page 21).

Castle Mini Cakes

EDIBLES
(per cake)

6cm (2³/₈") round cake, 6cm (2³/₈") deep (see recipes on pages 6–9)

30g (1oz) cake filling (see recipes on pages 10–12)

Sugarpaste (rolled fondant):

   90g (3oz) rose pink

   30g (1oz) green

   30g (1oz) pale pink

   5g (just under ¼oz) lilac

   A little white, black and dark pink

EQUIPMENT
(per cake)

Basic equipment (see pages 15–17)

10cm (4") round cake card

Square cutter: 1.5cm (½")

1   Cover the cake card with green sugarpaste and set aside.

2   Layer and fill the cake with the cake filling, then spread the remaining filling over the surface of the cake. Cover the top and sides of the cake separately with rose pink sugarpaste, following the instructions for the main cake to achieve a sharp edge.

3   Cut away a rectangle of sugarpaste from the front of the mini cake and fill the top half with a square of rolled-out black sugarpaste. Roll out some pale pink sugarpaste and cut out a piece to fit in the bottom of the stable door. Mark on a woodgrain effect in the same way as for the main cake then secure it in the gap.

4   Make smaller versions of the battlements, turrets, rooftops, shutters, flowers and the unicorn's head following the instructions for the main cake. Stick the unicorn's head to the black window with a little edible glue and hold in place until secure.

Templates

Monster Truck
pages 50-55

Princess Carriage
pages 72-79

Farmyard Fun
pages 80–91

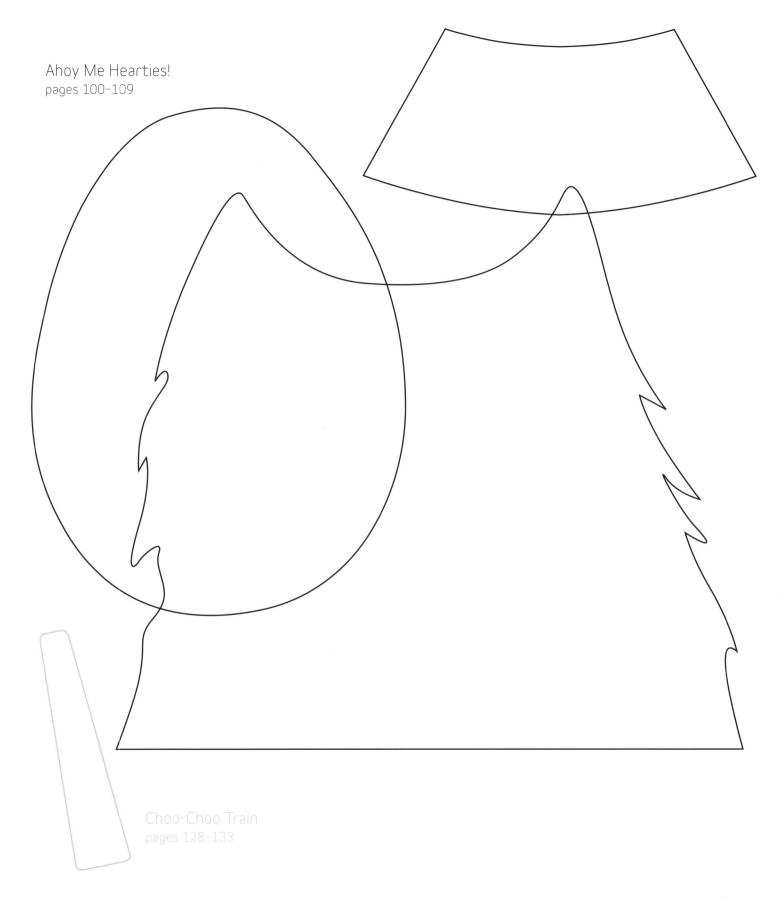

Ahoy Me Hearties!
pages 100-109

Choo-Choo Train
pages 128-133

Suppliers

Squires Kitchen, UK
3 Waverley Lane
Farnham
Surrey
GU9 8BB
0845 61 71 810
+44 (0) 1252 260 260
www.squires-shop.com

Squires Kitchen International
School, UK
The Grange
Hones Yard
Farnham
Surrey
GU9 8BB
0845 61 71 810
+44 (0) 1252 260 260
www.squires-school.co.uk

Distributors

UK

Culpitt Ltd.
Northumberland
www.culpitt.com

Guy, Paul & Co. Ltd.
Buckinghamshire
www.guypaul.co.uk

Squires Kitchen
Surrey
www.squires-shop.com

For your nearest sugarcraft supplier, please contact your local distributor.

Europe

Cake Supplies
Netherlands
www.cakesupplies.nl

Dom Konditera LLC
Belarus/Russia
www.domkonditera.com

Sugar World – Aliprantis Ltd.
Greece
www.sugarworld.gr

Tårtdecor
Sweden
www.tartdecor.se

Other books from B. Dutton
Publishing by Debbie Brown

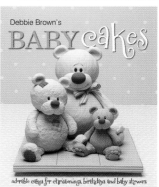

Other language editions available.

 B. Dutton Publishing is an award-winning publisher of cake decorating titles. To find out more about our books, follow us at **www.facebook.com/bduttonpublishing**.

  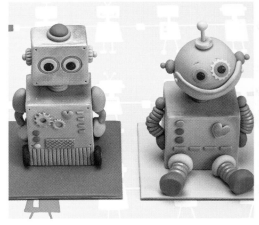